Curlers, Cows, & Kids

Fran Powers

All rights reserved. No part of this book may be used or reproduced by any means, graphic, electronic, or mechanical, including photocopying, recording, taping, or by any information storage retrieval system without the written permission of the author and publisher except in the case of brief quotations embodied in critical articles and reviews.

The illustrations used in this book are from the author and family members themselves.
Copyright 2014

"MAN WORKS FROM DAWN TO SETTING SUN
BUT WOMAN'S WORK IS NEVER DONE."

Dedication and Thanks to All

This book is dedicated to the Glory of God.

To my husband Hughes and his dairy cows, our four hyperactive children, Chuck, Marshall, David, and Tina. To my loyal beauty salon customers, the Powers and Tillery clans and all my Best Friends Forever. A very special thanks to Matt & Holly Newby and Eddie Lucas for their assistance and support of this book.

Contents

Foreword
Chapter 1: "What Do You Want to do When You Grow Up?"

Chapter 2: The Birth of My Beauty Salon.

Chapter 3: Anecdotes of a Dairy Farmer's Wife.

Chapter 4: Macho Mother: Mama Bird of the Boarding House Nest.

Chapter 5: Live and in Concert: This is Your Mother Speaking.

Chapter 6: Wow! Another Wild and Crazy Weekend at the Powers Boarding House.

Chapter 7: Games, Anyone?

Chapter 8: An Ole Worn out Athletic Supporter's Viewpoint.

Chapter 9: Hair Dresser.

Chapter 10: "Guess What I Did at the Beauty Salon Today?"

Chapter 11: How do you Keep them Down on the Farm After They've seen an Uptown Beauty Salon?
Chapter 12: Out Yonder in the Cow Pasture.

Chapter 13: Will the Real Troublemaker Please Stand Up?

Chapter 14: Those Muddy Little Rascals.

Chapter 15: Potpourri of Country Stuff and Things.

Chapter 16: Country Campaign Headquarters: Election Time Down on the

Farm.

Chapter 17: Occupational Hazards of a Beautician and a Dairyman.

Chapter 18: The Forgetful Booster Club President.

Chapter 19: The Godmother.

Chapter 20: What's Happening in the "Soaps" and Not in the Shampoos.

Chapter 21: "Dr. Fran's Holiday Rush Season Diet.

Chapter 22: What's a Few More Kids, Anyhow?

Chapter 23: Confessions of a Wacky Hairdresser.

Chapter 24: Patron for a Day.

Chapter 25: Beauty Show or Cow Auction: To go or not to go, that's the Question.

Chapter 26: Which Just Goes to Prove.

FOREWARD

For the past ten years I've been mixing curlers, cows, and kids daily. You see, while being a mother and wife of a dairyman, I also own and operate a beauty salon. What makes this especially unique is that the beauty parlor is within a stone's throw of my husband's milking parlor, located on our family's 200 acre dairy farm. The salon is an old frame white one story "cracker" farm house.

When I opened my beauty shop, I quickly learned to expect the unexpected that always seems to happen on a dairy farm. Even being an experienced farmer's wife and a beauty school graduate did not prepare me for the chaos that lay ahead.

No standard textbook of Cosmetology tells one how to raise children between shampoos and hair setting appointments and milking times. It seems that every five minutes or so my four kids covered from head to toe with black stinky mud will race through the beauty shop to the store room, swing open the refrigerator door and announce loudly that "there's nothing to eat." Then mumble, "There's nothing to do." My patrons' remark, "Sounds like an instant replay from home."

This book is a strange combination—dairy farming and hairdressing. Ours is a way of life, both simple and hilarious- one in which we share the best of both worlds.

Chapter 1

"WHAT DO YOU WANT TO DO WHEN YOU GROW UP?"

To go back to the beginning, as I recall nobody told me it would be this way. I have always been an early bloomer. By this I mean I was born, married and had a baby, all at the same time. At least, this is the way it seemed. This made me make the great decision, quickly, as to what I wanted to do when I grew up.

I had three choices – be a secretary, who would run around chairs and desks all of her life; a nurse, all in white, being chased by good-looking young interns; or a beautician, who would stand behind a chair for hours on end, making women beautiful. So I chose the latter. And now I find myself tending to the beauties as well as the beasts.

The next step was to find the perfect beauty school, or at least the one that would appreciate my talents (hidden to this date). Then, all I knew about hair was that you washed it when it was dirty, you cut it when it got in your eyes and mouth, and when all else failed, you went to a beautician who could remedy what you messed up.

After looking for a longtime (a full two weeks), I found the perfect school...Doodly's Hairstyling School. This house of higher learning was my home away from home for the next nine months, or 1200 hours, whichever came first.

Three other talented girls from my area also decided to further their education at the same beauty school. We got together and formed a car pool. Noth'in could stop us now!

Like four little calves being led to the slaughter, we didn't know what to expect.

THE ONE AND ONLY MRS. WATSON! To describe her is a task in itself. She was the stereotypical bleached blond. She missed nothing when it came to giving instructions on what "to do" and what "not to do," when you become a beautician. She had piercing blue eyes and a drill sergeant's voice. She was determined to teach us the fundamentals of making all women beautiful, and how to become rich and famous, in nine easy lessons.

The students were outfitted with the standard beauty equipment—white uniforms, white shoes, and "The Kit." The tool kit of our profession consisted of rollers, a shampoo cape, combs, brushes, manicure set, a set of permanent wave rods, end papers, clippies, a razor and scissors. All of these you had to monogram with your name in your favorite color. I chose red. This was to keep things straight for you and all of the other students... Until the day all the red colors got mixed together. You see, half of the class had picked red also.

"The Kit" became our third hand. It was a small black suitcase that went wherever we went. In fact, mine even slept with me. After a while I got to feeling like a doctor who was always on call.

Now that we had the equipment, as any unsuspecting new student would believe, we would start to use it—Wrong! Our morning lessons were spent studying theory. We soon were informed of the many names of great diseases, which we were sure with our knowledge we'd never catch. I got to wondering if I had enrolled in the wrong school as we had to learn names like Alopecia Areata, which means baldness in spots.

Meanwhile, I kept waiting for Mrs. Watson to teach the first lesson on how to make every woman beautiful and become instantly rich and famous. It didn't come yet. Even in the afternoon lessons, there were still no women to be beautified.

We worked on mannequins. Even so, there was always a mad race to get the ones with lots of hair. Our mannequins were plastic heads with implanted hair. This is why we called them the bodyless wonders, among other unmentionable names that we used on the ones that had bald spots or only three hairs on their entire heads.

One afternoon my luck had not completely run out and I ended up with the hairy one. I carried it around tucked under my arm and growled at the rest of the students like a dog with a big juicy bone.

On these bodyless wonders we learned our trade (loosely put). We pin curled, finger waved, wrapped permanent waves, sets and comb outs and learned how to cut.

Of course, we were not allowed to actually cut the hair because everyone knows that hair won't grow back on a plastic head. Basically I'm a swift person, but it wasn't until later that I finally realized that fact the hard way.

Before we could cut any type of hair at all, we first had to learn the right and wrong way to hold the scissors and comb together in one hand at the same time without cutting a thumb off.

It took me weeks to get the knack of it. Day and night I practiced until I was sure that I had grown twelve fingers to use for only this purpose.

Finally, when we mastered the art, we were ready to practice the directions of sectioning the bodyless wonder's hair and going through the motions of cutting it. A few of the students, myself included, went kind of hog-wild and cut away to our heart's content.

When we were finished we wondered what to do with the evidence so that no one would know who did it, especially our teacher, nosey Mrs. Watson.

After we tasted the not so new, well-preserved hair, we decided it needed a little dash of salt and, maybe, we could learn to like it after all. I can still taste the salty hair.

As we were progressing with our lessons, we had to learn the correct way to put a neck strip and shampoo cape on a patron without choking them to death or popping their eyes out. Even though our class received a gold star for not losing any patrons or their eyeballs, we still had several close calls on occasions.

One day our instructor, Mrs. Watson, gathered the flock of eager students around her beside the shampoo bowl. She held the sprayer hose in her hands and taught the lesson on the great art of shampooing.

In her command voice Mrs. Watson snapped, "Class you must first turn the water on and try to make it just right, not too hot or not too cold." One of the first lessons you learn either by experience or an early bath is that you hold tight to the rubber hose. It can be worse than a greased snake in motion for wetting anyone within its reach.

"Next it's very important to select the shampoo with the correct formula for the hair." "Now for the massage. Students, pay close attention and listen up." "At first you'll be afraid that you have a tender scalp and you will hurt your patron."

"Fear not students, for you'll find that more patrons have scalps like concrete and your body building exercises have helped for the amount of elbow grease you'll have to put behind most shampoos."

Mrs. Watson interrupted the lesson and boomed, "You students who are giggling will have a test tomorrow."

"Where was I," she said, "Oh yes, after a nice vigorous shampoo comes the rinse and this is tricky at best because it is unforgivable to get water in the patron's ears and eyes."

(During the rinse lesson I went out for recess and never had a makeup lesson because it seems I always get water where it's not supposed to be.)

Doodly's Hairstyling School taught a wide range of subjects, as well as a basic lesson in life. However, mine was how to survive in a carpool with four women drivers.

I have always blamed my problems with manicuring on the carpool. After I drove in the fast lane of traffic with the city slicker hot rod drivers and narrowly missed by a hair getting clobbered several times, I thought nails were to be chewed off instead of manicured.

My patrons couldn't stand the sight of blood when I clipped their fingernails too much. Before they fainted dead away I'd hurry and apply six coats of bright red polish on what was left of their nails so I could hide the gory sight from them.

Makeup lesson was fun. The girls would practice on each other, with so many new ideas that were concocted to make the face beautiful as possible. One memorable day I drew the class bully, Beulah, who shaved off my eyebrows, which meant that I had to draw the darn things on with a magic marker until I grew new ones. Everyone laughed and called me the class clown, including my instructor, Mrs. Watson.

Hair coloring class was always exciting and different, because every week you would have a different color of hair. Before I started Beauty School, I had, pardon the expression, virgin hair. This is hair that had never had tint applied to it. Well, my hair lost its virginity on the second day and I became a walking, talking rainbow like the rest of the class.

Now you must remember that all of this was taking place on either mannequins or students from the class. After acquiring the amount of hours and practice needed, we were ready to get our hands onto the real thing... a patron.

My first patron came for a haircut. I was scared. To think, here it was, the real thing and this courageous patron had put her hair into my hands.

After three hours of snip here and there, while under the constant scrutiny of my teacher, the patron told her that I had "just gone through the motions," held the scissors and comb just right, but I hadn't cut one hair off of her head. At this point the teacher told me, in unkind words, that I was to close the scissors together and cut. So I did, as I held my breath and closed my eyes.

I cut and cut until the woman had a neat plucked chicken haircut. When she looked in the mirror and viewed my handiwork, she screamed, "Scissor Happy!" I tool a liken to that nickname and decided to keep it from then on.

Next comes fun, fun, fun... The first time you are allowed to do hair color, again on a live patron... What should an instructor expect from a green beauty school student? Why, of course, green hair. Believe me, Mrs. Watson flipped out when my patron came up with light green hair.

A very good lesson, in fact, two lessons, was learned that day. First, is READ THE MANUFACTURER'S INSTRUCTIONS; and, I will never be a good chemist.

Sometimes Mrs. Watson and I didn't always agree on some of her ideas. Like the day when she stood me up in front of the whole class and shouted, "Powers, you will never become a beautician. You're the perfect example of a beauty school drop out." The class found it amusing and laughed their fool heads off. I did not. At that very moment, I knew I would never be the teacher's pet and personally could have cared less. All I wanted to do was dig a hole in the floor, crawl in it, and disappear.

There were times in class we could save face, by using someone other than a strange patron (they're all kind of strange, but I mean a stranger, of sorts). My first permanent was this kind of a challenge.

My sister, Shirley, was the brave girl to submit to my first attempt. She had just recently given birth to her first child, and she came carrying her soft little pillow to sit on for the lesson. Poor Sis didn't know what was in store for her.

I asked Shirley, "What kind of a permanent do you want, the over curled or the under curled?" She answered, uncomfortably, that she didn't care. Just hurry up and get to work.

First came the cutting, then the wrapping of the permanent wave rods. Funny thing, the rods kept falling out... so six hours later and after a lot of help from my classmates she was done, literally. When I helped Shirley out of the styling chair she said to us through clenched teeth, "I'll never forget this. I swear I'll get even with you when I get a hold of your hair one day."

A word of advice... DO NOT practice your beauty school lessons on your family, friends, or in-laws, because it is the quickest and easiest way to be disowned by each and every one of them. This, I didn't learn fast enough. Just ask my sister, Shirley.

Then there was my mother, who, bless her heart, went through this ordeal twice. The second time was with my kid sister, Debbie. With two hairdressers in the family it's a wonder Mother had any hair left on her head at all after we got through with practicing our homework lessons on her.

My 1200 hours completed, I was ready to graduate, without honors, but not before Mrs. Watson gave our class a farewell party and speech that did her proud. With her glib tongue and haughty manner, she said, "Students, I am very glad for each and every one of you to finally graduate. I believe this class had the lowest grades and the slowest learners in the history of this school."

With a glad farewell to our teacher and a sad farewell to our classmates, a nervous but happy goodbye to my car pool buddies, the next step was the State Board of Cosmetology Exam. This needed little sheet of paper would let us practice what we had been taught for the many preceding hours.

The instructor that gave us the big test made Mrs. Watson look like the "teacher of the year." A miracle happened. I passed my State Board Exam. They gave me the license with my name and number on it, proof that I was ready to go out into this big world and start to make every woman beautiful and me rich and famous.

Here I was, a fresh, green kid, right out of beauty school, diploma in hand, starting to look for a job. The first question asked by every shop owner was, "Do you have any experience?" How do they expect experience when the ink is still damp on my diploma?

Beating the pavements between shops brought me down to the last resort and the last shop. The owner felt sorry for me and hired me, I guess because I cried all the way through the interview. I was so happy and grateful that I kissed her stained hands all the way to her elbows.

During my first week I learned I wasn't prepared for the real world of beauty or the salon. Nobody told me it was going to be like this.

I soon discovered all the lessons and practice didn't mean you would be permitted to work on real live people. Instead, I became cleaning girl, stock girl, babysitter, nurse or given any other job that no one else wanted to do.

The first six weeks passed and I asked my boss how long before I could start to make women beautiful and become rich and famous? She laughed and then became hysterical and fell face first into the shampoo bowl.

I figured that I had better get started on my second dream, to own my own beauty salon. But that goal took more time than I envisioned.

During the next few busy years, working for someone else, I was getting "On the Job Training." There was no more stage fright. I was learning the hard way what life as a working hairdresser, standing behind the styling chair for hours and hours, was like. In other words, I got the leftovers (customers).

One day, in the middle of wrapping a permanent, I decided that I was prepared to take the giant step—my own Beauty Salon.

My search began to find the perfect, grand and elegant uptown building that would be my salon. It had to be a very chic, stylish, classy and sophisticated, super ultra-modern, Beauty Salon, I thought.

Every spare moment I had I searched for this location, between raising four children, plowing the north forty, slopping the pigs, feeding the chickens and helping my husband milk cows on the dairy farm.

Later, I was to discover my dream of a beauty salon was right there under my nose all the time on our family's farm. But, like all dreams, sometimes they can be nightmares, and I soon learned to take one madcap day at a time in my life as a wife, mother, and hairdresser.

Chapter 2

THE BIRTH OF MY BEAUTY SALON

For the next ten years, I learned what life was like in a Beauty Salon down on the farm. I found the perfect building on the ol'e homestead, it was owned by my father-in-law, and we agreed on the rent and needed repairs that made it into my dream of a beauty parlor.

The building was an old one-story frame "cracker" farmhouse, set up off the ground in the old time Florida fashion that once housed tenants who worked on the farm. Later, it had served as the location to buy the best cow manure around, just a little house with a great personality.

The yard had shrubs, blooming flowers and giant oak trees that sometimes would amaze you with a new family of something moving in and out of the landscaping, to add to the homey flavor, there were litters of different critters (cats, dogs, kids!!) roaming in and around the shop.

It didn't take long before I soon lost my "professional style" uniforms, and colorful smocks took their place. This was a habit that was a little hard to break after working in other salons, where they required the all-white uniform look.

Soon after that, I started the Farm-Styled Fashions or the Chic Country look. This meant blue jeans, stained white nurse's shoes and anyone of my favorite tee shirts. Some of them even helped advertise the dairy... phrases such as "Milk Drinkers Make Better Lovers" and "Drink More Milk." I even had one that said "Hairdressers do it with Style."

The one idea that I wanted everyone to get out of their heads was that I was a nurse. After being forced to wear white for many years, I was asked nearly every day, "Are you a nurse?"

The only questions I get now that I dress in my style is, "What are the milking hours?" and "How many cows do you feed?"

My husband refers to us as being a "two parlor family"—his milking parlor and my beauty parlor.

I knew in my heart that when this beauty salon was born, it was not going to be the average, everyday uptown beauty salon.

Opening day, my first customer walked through the front door (the door that still had the bullet holes from the last tenant, and the loose door knob), and I stepped up to her in my most professional tone and asked, "May I help you?" She stood there with a puzzled look on her face, looked around the room and finally said, "I want three bags of cow manure."

This request wasn't foreign to me as I had already had other people drive up and ask for the same thing and the telephone inquiries every once in a while.

Some of the men would go into shock, discovering they were in a beauty salon, and about break their necks running out of the door. A few people searched the entire beauty salon until they satisfied themselves that there were no bags hidden.

One thing about this location was that in giving directions all you had to say was, "Roll your windows down in the car—just follow your nose—when you smell the dairy farms, you'll know you're in the right place."

Once in a while someone who had been there before, but for a different reason, would say, "Oh, the white house that had the cow manure for sale."

My beauty shop's "city slicker" customers soon got used to the different barnyard sights, sounds and smells too, for they seem to delight in telling their friends that they got their done "next to the cow pasture."

The dairy farm had been owned by the Powers family for 45 years. The family consisted of Mr. and Mrs. Hershall Powers, who I called Granddaddy and Mother Powers. They lived right next door to the beauty salon. Fletcher, the older brother and his wife and four children, lived next to our house in the back pasture. Sister Doris and her husband lived in the house in the front pasture.

The dairy was located on 200 acres, in what used to be a rural area, between two small central Florida towns. But, as progress entered this area, there is now a four-lane highway facing it. My husband's family weathered many a storm in those 45 years in the dairy farming business. But in time, I soon learned that their dairy farm problems were my problems and my beauty salon problems were their headaches.

Chapter 3

ANECDOTES OF A DAIRY FARMER'S WIFE

I'll never forget the unforgettable day when I met my tall, dark and handsome Prince Charming named Hughes, and I swooned. It wasn't until the day after Hughes and I had tied the weddin' knot that I actually realized what extras were included besides him when I had said, "I do."

For starters there were 600 cows and a very large family. Being married to a dairy farmer must be a lot different than being wed to other farmers. First, I had to share my spouse with 600 cows, of which he had favorites and names. On occasion he even compared me to them! Also, my husband's very large family outnumbered the Hatfield and McCoy clans.

When I married Hughes, I became overnight kinfolk to half the folks in the county. I still haven't learned everybody's name. It seems I forever put the wrong face with the name. However, it really doesn't matter because they in turn just call me Hughes' wife.

In short order I learned what a dairy farmer's wife must know: (1) Dairy farmers get up very early in the morning. (2) They eat three <u>big</u> meals a day. (3) Wives and children are expected to help with the chores without bellyaching about it. (4) Dairy farmers come home for "recess" anytime of the day. (5) Cows behave like naughty children. If one cow does something wrong, they all follow: for instance, getting out of the pasture at 2:30 a.m. (6) Dairy farmers are on call 24 hours a day, 7 days a week, 365 days a year. Milk cows don't take the weekends and holidays off. Being a dairy farmer is not just a job—it's a way of life.

Of course, it wasn't all toil and no play. My husband made time between milkings to enjoy his hobbies – watching sports and going hunting and fishing. In my opinion his favorite pastime was telling bodacious stores about hunting and fishing and sports.

Once I suggested to my spouse to try my favorite hobby, day dreaming, explaining it can be enjoyed any place at any time and the best part is that it's free. My husband snapped, "Cripes, Fran, it's no wonder you act out-to-lunch most of the time. I'd rather just shoot the bull with my buddies."

Our fun time together as full-fledged dairy farmers consisted of sitting on our front porch in matching rocking chairs watching the cow's graze, the birds fly here and there, and the cornfields wave in the wind.

During this quiet time, conversations covered a variety of subjects ranging from the problems of my beauty salon customers, to his cows, to our children and families, and the never ending too wet or too dry weather problems.

The front porch conversations continued during our family vacations. It was the only topic that Hughes and I could remember to talk about after driving 500 miles non-stop, with four wiggling children and a nervous dog riding in the front seat of a pick-up truck.

On these torturous rides I would try to keep the kids busy looking at the scenery instead of punching a seatmate, namely me. I'd tell them, "Look, see the big black and white cows in the pasture? There must be a million in that herd out there. Why don't you kids count each one?"

The kids would hang their heads out the window for a look, then reply, "Who can count with Dad driving so fast? Anyway, our cows at home look a lot better."

Our family has also been known to take a bus-man's holiday with tours of dairy farms and beauty salons during our vacations.

When we would finally land at our appointed vacation designation, I'd fall out of the truck and kiss the ground on the spot where we'd stop.

Later, Hughes would relax and read his dairy farming journals, magazines, and seed catalogs.

For my reading time – between getting meals, washing clothes and refereeing four fighting off-spring, and one naught dog – I enjoy reading my all-time favorite, exciting and adventurous books, "The Sex Life of a Hair" volumes one and two.

Each summer, I'd keep my fingers crossed that my husband not get the bright idea to bring his favorite cow along with us on our vacation. Cows and kids in the front seat of a pick-up truck would be just too much!

But the kids would always manage to take their long hair along, and it would just happen to need cutting while on my vacation time. I'd tell them before each trip, "Do not pack your hair because I won't need it."

When it came time to tell our children about the birds and the bees or where babies come from, Hughes and I devised a way of keeping the message in tune with all of our lives. We told them about the bulls and the heifers. We thought it would be simpler than telling the kids about finding them under a cabbage leaf or a near-sighted stork brought them, or we ordered them out of the Sears and Roebuck wish book.

Most husbands' idea of an unexpected surprise is to send their wives flowers or to plan a birthday party in her honor. But my husband is much more original. His favorite surprise for me is to schedule the crop dusting plane to fly over our house repeatedly at 6:00 a.m. Then he gets very disappointed when I say I didn't appreciate his surprise.

To show the compassion my husband has for me, when I go hunting with him, he treats me like one of the boys and says, "If you kill it, you clean it." This is also the same rule he follows when it comes to fishing.

My husband's idea of a compliment is to say that he could pick me out of a room full of laughing people because, he says I was halfway in line between the mules and the pigs when it came to handing out laughs.

Just to show you that we are a very normal dairy farming family, we have a constant argument in our house that I discussed the other day with Carol, a friend, while she was over visiting and having a cup of coffee.

I told her, "Hughes cannot understand how a dairy farmer's house can run out of milk. He thinks it's a cardinal sin."

Carol said with amazement, "I thought you had a faucet in the sink that runs milk out of it."

"Oh, c'mon Carol," I said, "everyone thinks that. But it's not true."

"Anytime you run out of milk, rather than sneak into the supermarket wearing a wig, come to my house and I'll loan you a gallon." I sighed, "Thanks Carol, I'll keep that in mind. The only problem is that you live 3,000 miles away. I have a better idea than that." She asked, "To have a milkman deliver you a gallon of milk on your back doorstep?"

"I'm going to install a milk cow from the ceiling hanging over the kitchen bar and write each kid's name on her udder." "That's a great idea," said Carol, "I could use one at my house, too."

Later that day when I told Hughes my idea about solving the

milk shortage problem in our house he groaned, "Whose name would be put on the tail, because dummy that part doesn't give milk."

What would you think of a family that would drive their unclean, freshly used cattle truck to church on a very hot, humid day, parking it right in front of the front door, only to discover that the church windows were opened because the air conditioner was on the fritz? We found out that Sunday! Our family was the ones the sermon had been guided to. The topic was, "Cleanliness is next to Godliness."

Gifts—that's another novel way my husband has for showing me his love. For Christmas, anniversary, or birthday, I can nearly always depend on a season football pass, a milk bottle, a box of shotgun shells, a cow bell, a purple plastic fishing worm, a milk pail, a tractor tire, a beautiful green hunting jacket, or a pair of black knee-high rubber boots.

The latter does come in handy though, especially since we live in a cow pasture that during the rainy season sometimes gets impassable.

Whoever started the rumor that the life of a dairy farmers wife is peaceful and quiet had to be out of their ever lov'in mind. Thank goodness some naïve people don't believe every rumor they hear, unless they happen to be as crazy as I am.

Chapter 4

MACHO MOTHER: MAMA BIRD OF THE BOARDING HOUSE NEST

Like an over protective mother bird, I sat on the nest and hatched my first three children – Chuck, Marshall, and Tina. My fourth child, David, came the easy painless way. He came to dinner when he was 11 years old, and stayed.

Once a mother, always a mother, I quickly learned that even a mother bird must have a sense of humor and a heart of gold to raise her nest of offspring.

The children now have a new name for the nest, the Powers' Boarding House. Food is served 24 hours a day, 365 days a year, along with fun and games. It's a come as you are, free phone service, stereo and hi-fi, plus TV available, free laundry service, daily tours of the dairy farm, and "taxi" service available.

My kids have so many friends in and out that I hand out numbers when they come in the front door so, when their mothers call on the phone, I can page each number over the P.A. system. During a busy season at the Powers' Boarding House, when the kids run out of beds and floor space and start sleeping on the bed springs, I know it's time to put the "No Vacancy" sign on the front cow pasture gate.

Meal time at our house is like feeding time at the zoo in the middle of a three-ring circus, and everyone uses the boarding house reach at the table. My kids aren't hard to please. They'll eat anything as long as it's dead. And, they believe in calling for room service. They use the phone in the bedrooms to call the kitchen and ask, "What's there to eat?" or "When will dinner be ready?"

My mother once said that the kids remind her of a nest of baby birds waiting with their mouths open for the mother bird to feed them a worm. That gave me the idea to tell the kids that we were having "baked worms" for supper that night. Their response: "That's great, Mom!" By that time, I knew that they hadn't been listening anyway.

My parents get the courage to come for a visit about three times a year. Now, it's not that they live so far away – just five miles – but it takes them that long to get their nerves settled to try again after having been here the time before.

After we have what I consider a nice normal meal, Mother and Dad streak for the door ready to leave the bedlam behind. All the way to the car they're saying, "We don't know how you stand it. We'll call you on the phone after we have recuperated."

In their departing cloud of dust, they can hear me saying, "Stand what, Mother and Dad? I'm just getting paid back for the mean things both Hughes and I did when we were mean little kids."

I wonder why it is that children and animals go together like peanut butter and jelly. Because, I guess, they stick together... animals and kids everywhere, and not a one that works. They just sleep all day, until it's feeding time or their favorite TV program comes on.

The last livestock count at my house was three dogs, (one inside and two outside), seven cats, (six out, one in), one huge rabbit named "Snowballs" (sometimes inside and sometimes outside), three horses (limited to being on the porch, or inside the garage) and 600 cows that go about anywhere they want to. But they usually play havoc with the lawn, both by eating everything in sight and fertilizing it.

The swimming pool has been the big watering hole for all the animals, not only ours, but an array of uninvited guests. My kids always enjoy playing the guessing game of, "Mother, guess who's in the swimming pool today?" When they say "who" instead of "what," I feel a certain wave of relief, but when they say "what," I figure, "Okay kids, I'll play your silly games" and start with the phrase, "Is it alive?" Their answer verifies that "it" is very much alive, and a very good swimmer. So I start down the list: "Is it a rat, but, turtle, frog, duck, fish, snake, raccoon, possum, or an alligator?" They start with the riotous laughter and say, "Who told you?"

Not knowing which one I had hit the jackpot on, I go for myself and check out who the uninvited guest is. Last time this happened, I exclaimed, "Get that alligator out of that pool, or so help me I'll feed you kids, one at a time, to it for its lunch!"

At this point, I feel like posting a sign beside the pool saying, "Enter at your own risk; not responsible for any and all surprises you may encounter."

I have contributed the problem of having my voice being mistaken for Tina's, due to the fact that I am under the constant strain and emotional stress of figuring "what's next." But how do I explain that to people I have known all my life who mistake my voice on the phone for my very own mother. They say, "Like mother, like daughter."

When I was growing up, my Mom would sometimes call me by the wrong name, which, at the time, I thought was very funny. There were four girls in our family, so eventually we hit on the number identification. I happened to be lucky number two; and Mom, if she could get the attention of number one, would stop there and Shirley was the one that was asked first to do a task. This worked until number one found that if she didn't answer, mother would go on down the line and one of us was bound to answer, not realizing what was going on.

I am going through the same "phase" now, only I'm in worse condition than poor Mom. I call the kids and the animals by the wrong names so whatever task I had on my mind to begin with gets lost in the shuffle of kids and animals, names and numbers, and I end up doing it myself, or telling them, "Heck, you know who you are even if I don't." Maybe that is the reason why I call the Vet's office to check if the children have had their measles shots, and the doctor to ask if the animals distemper shots are due.

Two of my four children call me Mom or Mother. The other two call me "Cool Breeze" and "French Toast." Why, I'm not real sure. Guess it's because that is their "favorite" – a nice cool breeze. Of course, Marshall, liking to eat all the time, calls me, "French Toast." I take this as a compliment or a loving expression. Maybe I shouldn't ask too many questions, my balloon may burst! I have been referred to as "Oh, you know her" when they are conducting a sight-seeing tour enroute to the refrigerator.

Being the middle child of a mother who is also a middle child, could explain my son, Marshall's unusual behavior. Forgetfulness should have been his middle name. He forgets everything he owns and every place he goes, including himself. It takes every member of the family, plus all the King's horses and all the Dairy's cows to keep up with Marshall's belongings and Marshall.

People refer to, "losing your head if it wasn't attached"; that suits Marshall to a tee. I wouldn't be a bit surprised if he called me on the phone from school telling me that he was missing something he needed for the next class, namely his head, and ask me if maybe I could run it down for him as he was going to need it for a few of his classes. His suggestions to where it could be is "under the bed, in the closet, or maybe he lost it when he came out of the house on his way to school." Seems like he had it on at breakfast this morning..."

When I was pregnant with Marshall, it seems to me that my doctor told me I could do almost anything without affecting the baby. Little did that doctor know what affects painting a barn from atop a 30-

foot ladder, and climbing to the top of the feed silo, has had on Marshall!

In our house, instead of "One Life to Live," our soap opera is "Four Lives to Live." Our four children could put most of the soap yarns to shame when it comes to love affairs. By this, I mean they change characters once a day instead of just every once in a while. If you miss one chapter, usually in a couple of hours, you have hardly a chance of ever catching up.

Dating. That is the ultimate for the parent who has a child going out on his first date. First, there are the preliminary efforts that are expended before the mirror making sure they look their very best. Then the anxious hours that the parents sit waiting for them to come home and give the complete run down, blow by blow, of this momentous occasion.

Hughes and I had an idea what our answers would be – okay, alright, or fine – but, we figured, with all of the enthusiasm that preceded this date, maybe we were in for a surprise. When the kids came in, we were waiting with baited breath to ask all the questions that got the pat answers of "okay," "alright" and "fine". When we figured out that this was all we were going to get, we improvised, "How was your dinner with the Queen?" The reply was, "Okay." "How was the ticker tape parade in your honor?" "Alright", and last, "How was your trip around the world?" With this last answer, we knew that we weren't going to be included in on his date, be it good or bad.

One of the most profound questions a parent can ask his child is, "Do you love me or my car?" Having three driving children and one that still rides, our family is forever playing "musical cars." In our game, when the music stops, whoever isn't in a car and gone, gets to stay at home. I've told the kids to call and make an appointment for my car, which happens to be the newest one on the "Powers Used Car Lot."

Excuses have hit all highs on originality for using a car other than your own. Chuck asked to use the car and I asked him, "What's the matter with yours?" He said, "Nothing, except my car is a day car; it won't run at night."

David came right up behind Chuck's explanation that his car had a flat time, "Could I use the pick-up truck?" The answer was "No."... to the truck, the car, the tractor, the feed truck and even the cattle truck. He finally got down to the dragline and the bulldozer. Finally he said, "Can I use the horse?" His Dad said, "Ask your mother."

Chapter 5

LIVE AND IN CONCERT: THIS IS YOUR MOTHER SPEAKING

Since prehistoric times, (which is also the time in which my kids think I was born), mothers have given their children the same instructions to follow day after day. This goes on until the mother either wears out of the birds fly out of the nest.

To save myself on all this nerve wracking repetition, I have threatened for years to make a tape recording of me "Live and in concert" and play it to my children every day. With the tape recording doing the mothering job, I would have more free time to practice yodeling the cows in from the pasture for their milking time, or read a whole sentence in a book without being interrupted.

The tape would play two parts – part one, morning instructions, and part two, night-time instructions. On the part one, morning instructions would be the following messages played on the highest volume of the tape recorder:

"Attention, this is your mother speaking! Now hear this! This tape will not self-destruct after playing the following messages, but instead will continue replaying 327 times or until you get the message through your hard heads.

"Wake up, you're late already. For the last time, get out of bed or you'll miss your bus. Get dressed, eat your breakfast, hurry up and brush your teeth, comb your hair, pick up your clothes, clean your room, make your bed, HURRY UP YOU'RE LATE!" "Don't forget the items you're supposed to take to school today, as I will not bring forgotten items to you. (Customers don't like their heads left in the shampoo bowl while I run off to school.)" "Hurry up the bus is coming. Goodbye! DO NOT ERASE PART 2 OF THIS TAPE OR I WILL BREAK YOUR ARM."

Part 2: Night instructions would go like this... "Pick up your school books, put your clothes and shoes away, do your homework, do not eat yet, turn the radio down, get off the phone, do your homework, eat your supper, take your bath, brush your teeth, turn off the radio and the TV. Did you do your homework, turn off your lights, for the last time go to sleep and good night!"

I know what would happen if I ever made such a tape. After hearing yesterday's famous tape recording of children's daily instructions played, I would have to search the house to find the missing mother's helper and finally question four guilty looking children. "All right, which one of you dorkies ate my tape?"

THE FAMILY ENTERTAINMENT CENTER.

Most normal people entertain in their family rooms, or rec-rooms, around the pool, or in their living rooms. Our children's favorite room is none of the preceding rooms, not even their own bedrooms. When they want to have a ball, they come into Hughes' and my bedroom. Their explanation for this is that "the TV in our bedroom works the best, and besides, your bed is the biggest."

It's a case of first there, first served. My husband and I have to climb over kids and animals to get to our bed in our bedroom. It makes no difference whether we know the kids, or the animals, we have a crowd. In fact, we have missed the jist of many a good TV show during a shift of bed "characters." Heads, feet, and rumps are a little hard to see through, seeing that I didn't take Hughes suggestion: "If you would have made our kids out of glass when you were sittin' on the nest." At this remark, I told him that it takes two.

When we have all of this togetherness time, the kids think it's real cute to say, "It's 11:00, do you know where your children are?" I know where I would like for them to be, but good mothers don't talk like that...

LONG HAIR OR SHORT.

The Powers children were in style long before the rest of the country. They had the long, shaggy look. Many friends and relatives would hint to me about our long-haired kids and my only comment would be, "They could call for an appointment, but I refuse to work at 11:55 p.m. on Friday, or 7:10 a.m. on Sunday morning." Now you try and keep up with a family like that. They seemed to have a sixth sense, that if they waited long enough, they would be right in style, and they were right – only 17 months passed the last time.

Their father finally got the message across to them that they were all going to have their day in the styling chair. His persuasion came with the sharpening of his pen knife. I had stalled him as long as possible with the explanation, "I love the new style. We have real trend setters in the Powers family." I went on to say, "I even think it's COOL."

That was all he needed to hear. The appointment time was set for 5:15 p.m. in our back yard. Each kid, in their turn, was run down, tackled, dragged back to the chair and tied securely.

At this point, I told them they could do with me just what my patrons do when they come into the beauty salon – tell me about their love life, or their friends' love lives. And, then, I made the fatal mistake. I asked them how they wanted their hair cut.

Knowing that this was an unreal question to be asked by ones hairdressing mother, they still tried to get their point across that they just wanted a trim, not a cut. Of course, I did what I wanted with their tresses.

David was the first in the chair for his cut. He said, "Mon, I want my hair cut just like Billy's; you know who I mean, the one that looks like he came from outer space."

When I stopped to think for a minute, that is exactly where he went to get that style, "The Outer Space Beauty Salon" so my reaction was "No, we don't copy the competition."

My patience was worn to a frazzle by the time I was down to the fourth kid (3 hours and 46 minutes later). All I could hear was, "Just a little trim, just a little off the ears" (oh, what a temptation that was). This kid wiggled and squirmed, but I kept on cutting. Finally, when I was finished at my wits end, I thought to myself, it's not fair... when I go through this at the beauty salon on a paying teenager, they can go home and gripe to their parents. Being both their hairdresser and their mother, I have to hear morning, noon and night, what a terrible thing I had done to them.

Living with four unhappy complaining, short haired children are no way to keep peace of mind at home or at work. I told them, in hopes that they would hush, that: (1) non-paying and non-tipping customers have no right to complain, (2) the ones with a bowl-cut look, are not to tell anyone who cut it, (3) the lucky ones that came up with the "In Style," should tell all of their friends where they get it styled, (4) if you are real unhappy with your hairdresser go to another one, (5) do not ask for free hair advice on the spur of the moment and, finally, (6) if you go to another hairdresser, your mother will cry and you will have a terrible time explaining that to your friends, so there.

I am the perfect example of what brain-washing can do to a person's mind. Living with a house full of children, I pick up their strange language that sounds like a foreign tongue to my ears. Whatever new words or phrases enter into this house is taken up by me in a couple of days. The only bad thing is that I start to use them on my customers within a few days after hearing them. I have a hard time, sometimes, explaining after I have greeted one of my older, refined patrons with, "hey man" or "what's happening, momma" followed by, "You know, you're a real cool chick." But I believe the worst blooper I made was calling one a "Turkey" and the other one a "Dog."

On the whole, my kids' vocabulary keeps me from being at a loss for words to use on my patrons. Most of the time, as I am practicing the latest dance step behind my styling chair while answering their crazy questions, I come up with words like really, gosh, gee-whiz, it's a drag, yeah, gross, what's happening, out of sight, it's the pits, cool, give me five, or see you later.

Each member of my family has their favorite music to listen to. So I hear hard rock, country, disco, and country rock playing at the same time on different radios. The cars and trucks, the minute you open the doors, blare at you. But the music doesn't stop there. The cows in the barn have to listen to music on the radio while they are being milked. What is it they say about "contented cows?" They have their favorite music too, and get rather upset if it's not the right kind of entertainment.

At least the cows have a silent time in their lives. At night, I wake up to four different kinds of music going all at one time while the kids are sound asleep in their beds. But don't ever turn them off, because the minute you do, each kid, in turn, wakes up and says, "I was listening to that" or "what's there to eat?" So the lesser of two evils is to turn the music back on, or go to your bedroom, cover your head with a pillow and try to go to sleep. Even listening to the most requested, number one song of the day is hard to digest when you hear it played four different ways on four different radios. But I found that it is easier than trying to feed the "troops" in the middle of the night.

In this household, the habit of borrowing has brought up an idea that would revolutionize the world – The Eleventh Commandment: Thou shall not borrow from your parents. This would include money, cars, clothes, or camera. Nothing is more frustrating than to know where you have put something, just to go there and find that someone in the family has borrowed it and not told you.

A few incidents when this happened made me doubt my sanity. My daughter, Tina, and I share a love for horses and horseback riding. On one occasion, she let her enthusiasm get carried away. One whole weekend, her mare, Velvet, spent a fun-filled weekend in the pasture with a super stud, which we thought for sure in time she would become a mother.

Tina couldn't wait till she got to school to tell everyone, including her teacher, that we were going to have a new baby at our house. Not realizing what had transpired at school, I soon began getting telephone calls inquiring about my health.

After being called by Tina's teacher for a conference at school, I was standing at Mrs. Pell's desk and she asked me to sit down and have a visit.

"How are you feeling now a days," Mrs. Pell asked. I answered, "Fine, thank you."

She said, "You are looking so well, and I notice that you haven't gained any weight yet."

Not knowing what that was all about, I told her that she looked real good, too.

She said, "Tina told me your wonderful news and she is so excited she can hardly wait."

I had warned her not to tell anyone, until we knew for sure, but now I knew that she had had a slip of the mouth.

Mrs. Pell said to me, "Well, you know how children are about a new arrival; they can't wait to tell their friends about it."

I said, "Yes, she's wanted a new one for so long, that's all she talks about. She wants one to raise and spoil rotten."

"What do you want, a boy or a girl?"

"I really don't care, as long as it's healthy."

"When is the baby due?" she asked.

"In about 11 months," was my answer.

"11 months! Are you sure? I thought it only took 9 months to have a baby."

"A BABY!" I exclaimed. "I'm not going to have a baby. Tina's horse is having a foal."

Arguments and fighting kids: They are a plague to a working mother.

Trying to settle a fight or argument over the phone, when the kids know they are safe from a spanking, is nearly impossible, plus very nerve racking. My children know the perfect time.

At times, I swear they are telepathic, because I will start a shampoo, with my hands wet, full of shampoo, my customer's head in the shampoo bowl, and the telephone starts to ring off the hook. I have to wash off the shampoo, leave my customer hanging in the sink, answer the phone and listen to the latest argument.

"Mom, this is Tina. Tell Marshall to get off my back. "I tell her,

"Let me talk to Marshall. Marshall, get off your sister's back. Bye."

Back to the lady's head in the sink. I turn on the water, the phone rings. I turn off the water; answer the phone with wet hands. "Mother, tell Marshall to give me back my tape recorder. He hid it and won't tell me where it is," came Tina's voice, loud and clear. "Let me speak to Marshall."

Trying to be calm and professional, "Marshall, give your sister's tape recorder back to her, and stop teasing because I'll know it if you don't." His retort was, "How will you know?" "Because Tina will tell me," I said.

Once again I go back to my customer's wet soapy head to finish what I was so rudely interrupted two times, so far. Most of the time, I hang the phone under my chin and do my scolding that way, because I usually have to hear at least four different versions of the same quarrel, and I waste a lot of time if I stand at the desk all the time. When it begins, I put the telephone in the shampoo bowl and leave it there until time to close the shop at the end of the day. I have thought about leaving it there all summer long or at least until school starts and the kids are back in school.

"The Empty Nest Syndrome," that is what every parent suffers when their children go off to college for the first time. I had two Baby Birds leave at the same time. I would go to the beauty salon and cry to my customers that my babies had flown away, and I didn't know how I could stand having them gone "out of the nest."

Many of the ladies had gone through the same syndrome and told me, "Dry your tears. They'll be home on the weekend with a bundle of dirty laundry for you to do."

I tried to listen to these words of wisdom and the first weekend was my complete belief in "higher learning." Not knowing what was in store for me, I went home from the salon, armed with a super big box of detergent ready to face the mountains of dirty clothes I knew were awaiting me. To my surprise when I opened the door, I heard the boys comparing laundry hints and detergents. And there wasn't a dirty piece of clothing to be found in their luggage. They told me that since I would never be the award winner of "The cleanest, brightest, softest, wash test" and they had decided to take a "crash" course in "How to wash laundry, the modern way." So, on and on they went, explaining the pros and cons of their favorite detergent.

My next day proved to be equally as enlightening. Arriving home after a particularly hard day at the beauty salon, I opened the door and found son, Chuck, ironing his shirt to wear for his date that evening.

First surprise was I didn't remember having an iron. Thought I had given it to the church's rummage sale 13 years ago. The only iron that I gave a thought to was in a vitamin tablet.

Son, David, was not to be out done. There he sat with a needle and thread, mending his clothing. So, I asked him if he was for hire, he could start on mine.

Monday morning at the beauty salon, after the "weekend shock," I couldn't wait to tell my customers that I was very impressed with "higher education" and the courses my sons were taking would be a definite help, later on, in "How to find a wife."

During a Sunday sermon at our church, I overheard my third son trying to explain to a new friend of his why I was the only one standing up. He said, "It's occupational, she's a hairdresser, and she can only listen when she is standing." Little did I realize, until that moment, that I could listen only when I was on my feet.

Standard equipment with each kid in our house is a blow dryer for their hair. I not only have to hear the dryers at the salon all day, but all four, in high pitched harmony, during my time off at home.

Another disgrace that most everyone in the profession has is never a comb or a brush or shampoo to be used at home.

Now, I know how my dairy farmer feels when he has no milk for his cereal in the morning.

Chapter 6

WOW! ANOTHER WILD AND CRAZY WEEKEND AT
THE POWERS BOARDING HOUSE

God has built a beautiful system, with a season for all things. The seventh day of the week the Lord made for man and woman to rest – (unless a cow falls in the ditch and needs to be pulled out, or there is a hairdresser's show to attend).

The weekend. A time when everyone takes the bull by the horns and pursues their favorite pastimes of work or play. A time when the city folks head for the country, sometimes with camper in tow, on a back-to-nature jaunt and the simple life. And, the country folks sample a taste of the hustle and bustle of city life.

Thank goodness it's Saturday, was my biggest thought while I turned the "Closed" sign in the window of the beauty salon. It had been a real horse race of a day and I was thinking, "Another day, another dollar, another day older and deeper in debt. Maybe next week my tractor will come in, loaded with money and I can retire in a manner in which I would like to become accustomed to and give up this 9 to 5 work habit."

During the minute I stood by the door, I couldn't decide which part of me ached the most – my back, arms, tongue, or my feet. Even my face hurt from the smile that I had to wear all day. Just then I couldn't breathe, due to the fact I had on a brand new pair of extra heavy duty support stockings that had cut the circulation off in the middle of my body around what used to be my waist, which in turn had caused my varicose veins to turn white. I looked down at my poor swollen, tired feet and said, "Feet, don't fail me now, at least until I can get home and take off my work shoes."

Locking the beauty shop door securely, I slowly walked to

my car and thought of my exciting plans for the weekend. A Sunday afternoon nap!

I am a firm believer in the weekend nap pastime, come whatever. Like Goldilocks, I can be found fast asleep in someone's empty bed, someplace in our house.

My energetic, wide eyed, bushy tailed family complains loudly about me hibernating like a bear and treats me like a coiled rattlesnake or an uncaged hungry lion. I tell them, "So what, if I growl or roar when I wake up from my forty winks or strike out at anyone or thing that moves in my path."

With each Sunday afternoon comes the promised uninterrupted nap, which I am convinced is only a dream away, never to be finished. Even my before-nap prayers don't seem to help.

I remain steadfast and determined in my quest for the perfect peaceful slumber in the middle of "Grand Central Station." With my head covered with two pillows and a blanket, I simply pass out from lack of oxygen and have no need to count sheep to go to sleep.

Over the years, I have kept a checklist of my family's reactions when I announce to them that I am going to take a nap. First, they get a faraway look in their eyes, while they're promising to be quiet as a dead mouse while I sleep. As certain as twice a day milking times, my family will start their pre-nap warm up exercises then continue through my entire nap time.

They slam doors, develop quick cases of whooping cough, turn on every appliance in the house, tell all the dogs to bark and the cows to moo. In the kitchen, everyone acts like a Bull in a China shop. They talk, whistle, sing, hum, sneeze, and laugh; stage a yelling, screaming, running fight through the house; flush toilets, turn on the shower, tell every person this family has ever known, plus my mother to call on the phone; invite half of the folks in the county over to cheer for the winning team on TV as if there was a million dollars bet on the game, even if it's not the Super Bowl or the World Series; practice the piano, trumpet, drums and guitars; play games in the house, chase, You're It, Hide and Seek, Simon Says, touch football, basketball, soccer, Frisbee-throwing, bowling, tag, wrestling, tennis, golf, ping pong and pool; practice roller skating, fishing, skateboarding and dancing.

One Sunday afternoon, during my family's nap exercises,

I woke up like a giant to a buzzing noise in my ears. My first googled thought was, I found the tooth fairy hidden under the pillows, where I covered my head to black out the noise. I soon discovered the buzzing noise didn't come from the tooth fairy, but two breath-holding, blue faced insects – one a fly, the other a mosquito. "Another one bites the dust," I said as I slammed the pillow down on the insects.

I lay in bed, in a semi-conscious zombie state listening to the noisy, mad house full of nuttier than fruit cake group of people outside my bedroom door and decided, Lordy, it's no wonder I'm jumpy as a bed bug all the time. Then I thought about what my husband had said to me. "You're not getting any younger. Maybe you do need a nap after all."

Some beauty rest! My face was wrinkled from the pillows, one arm was still numb, my hairdo was a wreck, my mouth was dry from no air under the pillow and my eyes were swollen shut.

Again, I thought, time to rise and shine. Slowly I crawled out of bed yawning and stood up to stretch my bones, then I peeked out of the window to view the surrounding familiar landscape. I gasped at the sight. There were crazies and loonies running around our cow pasture in pickup trucks, jeeps, dune buggies, motorcycles, go carts and cars.

The waiting line of traffic leading to our house was bumper to bumper. The lane had a crowd that any drive-in movie would envy on dollar night.

"Where is the No Trespassing Sign?" I yelled to my husband. He asked, "Why do you want the sign?"

"I want to put it on the gate in the front cow pasture to keep those fools out."

"What fools?" he said.

"The ones in the cow pasture playing demolition derby with their noisy vehicles."

My husband said as he looked out the window, "This rain brings out the mudslinging enthusiasts every time. When the mud dries up they disappear."

At that moment a truckload full of redneck yahoos scratched off in our front yard where the grass used to be growing and a man on a motorcycle rode on the new dirt track.

"Where is that No Trespassing Sign," I said angrily.

"Remember last week when I ran the hippies out of the pasture for gathering the wild mushrooms?"

I said, "Yes."

"Well, the hippies ate the mushrooms along with the No Trespassing Sign," said Hughes.

I asked, "Did you tell the hippies about my idea of a money making project for the PTA that you vetoed?"

My husband said, "No, I didn't. They left so fast I didn't have a chance. I've already told you there's no way the PTA group can have a rock concert in my cow pasture and have you offer haircuts at half price. But I'll change my mind if they will put on a Country and Western music concert."

Later, when my kids told me that concerts usually last two days on the weekends, and that meant during my Sunday afternoon naptime, I quickly forgot my money-making idea for the PTA.

Many years ago my mother said to me, "You deserve to be a Farmer's wife and live in the peaceful countryside on a dairy farm. It would be good for your nervous condition to live on the cow's side of the fence where everything is quiet and restful."

To this day I've yet to fully understand what my mother really meant by her statement.

Chapter 7

GAMES, ANYONE?

My husband is the official recreation director of the Powers Boarding House. He is never at a loss for different games to suggest for the guests to play.

To add a little excitement and get the old adrenalin flowing, my spouse will simply call a game a contest. Then watch out. It's every man, woman or child for themselves. The winner, or maybe winners, of the contest are easy to pick out of the crowd. They are the ones with one finger on their hand, held high in the air, saying, "We're number one."

"It's not whether you win or lose, but how you play the game that counts," was once said by a losing coach before he was fired.

Now, the losers can be spotted with their heads hung low, shoulders slumping. They are supposed to be good sports and show the true meaning of sportsmanship at the end of a game. But they shouldn't make nasty remarks to the winners like, "I don't want to play with you anymore, you're no fun. You don't play fair, you cheat."

Which in turn the winners' remarks are, "Sorry you weren't up to par for the game. Too bad, you really gave it all you had. You really played a good game. Better luck next time."

The location of a contest makes no difference to my husband and the boarding house guests. To them, the inside of the house is as good as the outside. When the location inside the house has been selected for the game, I then enter the game and call a "Time out". I give everyone the two minute warning, then I tell them to go outside and play.

With a yard the size of a football field, each one should have plenty of room to do their own thing. They could really get down to business of letting the best man win.

One day during a rough and tough game of tug-of-war, with the rope stretched through the length of the house that had lasted without a letup for what seemed like hours, with each opposing team fighting to hang on to the bitter end, I thought, if no one else needed a rest, then I sure did. So, calmly, I asked the members of both sides if anyone wanted to play a game of marbles, or join me in a hand of cards? How about a puzzle? Maybe a quick game of jacks? Anyone for paper dolls? You want to color with my new crayons in my neat Burt Reynolds coloring book? Anyone for looking at my bubble gum cards with the cow pictures on them? Does anyone want to see my collection of dried hair clippings?"

From either side came no takers to my offers. They only looked at me with strained faces and pulled on the rope harder. A little snip with my scissors right in the middle of the rope ended the tug-of-war game. Both teams booed me while they dashed out of the house to the front lawn.

"Can Mr. Powers come out and play?"

There stood little Donnie looking up at me like an angel. "If he's a good boy and cleans up the mess in the house," I said.

A little while later I said to my husband, "Close the door! Were you born in a barn?"

"Yes," he said, and slammed the door.

From years of experience, the outdoor games in the yard are ones I excel in and play the best.

I trained regularly to maintain my form to stay in topnotch condition to participate in my special sports activity – observing. Through years of strict practices and outstanding dedication, I have finally earned the title "Super Fan" at the boarding house, which comes from me having to watch someone do something while I cheer them on.

At times, being a "Super Fan" title-holder is one that all mothers share while raising their children. We get in a rut, then we develop a habit of when he hear a kid yell, "Hey Mom, watch this," we pause, whether the kid is ours or not and watch. This habit remains even when we become a grandmother.

Once everyone is out in the yard, I settle myself in my favorite front row seat – the rocking chair on the porch –and await the start of the games and to watch the new winners and losers of the contests. In our games to settle a tie, the players go into sudden death overtime of drawing straws.

To name a few of the games played on the lawn are football, soccer, tennis, volleyball, badminton, basketball, throwing horseshoes, lawn darts, and croquet.

From time to time there are different shows staged on the lawn for entertainment. A horse show, or an animal show, or a rodeo.

Sometimes my husband and the boarding house guests will continue their games in the cow pasture.

He has to caution new players to watch where they step and always step high to be on the safe side. Also, to watch out for the stinging nettles and the beggar lice plants and the fresh piles of cow manure.

Out yonder in the cow pasture baseball field during a game with the bases loaded in the first inning, one barefoot swift player giggles when the brown stuff oozed between his toes. My husband just laid it on them about the players not kicking the bases and whatever they do, "Don't slide!"

The most unique golf tee is a dried pile of dung. That is one way you are very careful to keep your head down and watch the ball, because a low shot can become disastrous to a clean outfit. The obstacles in a cow pasture would challenge Arnold Palmer. One good rule is to always yell, "Four" regardless of who is playing the game ahead of you. Gopher holes, pot holes, water holes and sand traps make the game very interesting. Another rule in "Cow Pasture Golf," always use a club to locate your ball when it can't be seen.

For the boarding house guest that prefers water sports, my spouse, the recreation director of the boarding house, suggests boating and water skiing in the cows' watering hole out in the North Forty.

Also, out in the cow pasture, a noisy tractor-pulling contest is an attention getter, followed by the horse, car, and motorcycle races. The sport of track and field events with the runners and bike races dodging fence posts and cows to end the victor.

Every time I watch a crowd of people around me, it happens, the hairdresser in me comes out. Sometimes it can be a drag, but I just can't help it. Visions of dirty-haired, prospective beauty shop customers appear all around me. I look at a person and before I realize it, I'm styling their hair in my mind's eye.

For instance, from my front row seat on the porch, I can see one of the boarding house guests turning cartwheels and hand stands on the lawn. She would look so much better with a shorter hair style and could see where she was going without that thin limp hair in her face. Poor girl, her hair has no body and it's in terrible condition. The ends look like a kitten sucked on them and that mousy dishwater blonde color has got to go. Bless her heart, she needs help. I would give my eyeteeth to lighten her hair to a light color and add subtle tones of blond to enhance her beauty.

Oh, wait, there's a dark haired boy over there practicing his barb wire fence jumping with his Bozo the Clown hair style sticking out from under his baseball hat. I would just love to run my fingers through his hair first with the comb and then the scissors. I know there is a real hunk of a man under all that hair.

I would be in hog heaven if I could get hold of that man with a pig tail, hanging down the middle of his back, or the little red-haired girl with the home hair cut done with pinking shears.

To satisfy the hairdresser in me, I hand out my business cards to the boarding house guests, while I tell them all about the beauty shop I go to, and personally recommend there is no job too big or small. It's a full service beauty salon, staffed with experts, where all of your beauty and hair care needs are filled, open six days a week, evenings by appointment -- walk-ins welcome.

"Are you finished giving your business talk to our guests?" asked my red-faced spouse after he won the sack race.

"Yeah, I'm finished now. Do you want to go for a walk with me to stretch your legs a bit?" I asked him.

"No, I'm busy," huffed my spouse.

As I walked down the lane, I heard my husband shout to the other enthusiastic mob of participants, "The last contestant in the pasture for the mud wrestling contest has to get the cows into the barn for milking."

Chapter 8

AN OLE WORN-OUT ATHLETIC SUPPORTER'S VIEWPOINT

After seven long years, Hughes is now retired from amateur coaching of football, basketball and baseball, due to the fact that I lost his coach's whistle in the washing machine.

I knew it was bound to happen sooner or later the way I cram everything together in the washer. As I remember, he raised a real hoopty-doo when I laid it on him about the news of his whistle.

Instead of being a contented bench warmer, I joined my husband and sons at their sports play and became a water girl, coach's wife and a tired dragged out mother.

To the complaining wife of the sports fan, I say, "Relax, kiddo. Imagine being the coach's wife." Having put in my time of duty, I know.

I not only sacrificed my husband's time to his cows, but to his team for seven years. I was den mother for the team. I worried about each and every one of them as if they were my own. I'd watch them through many a dull practice and hope and pray that no one got hurt during the game. I'd talk to them when they were down and laugh with them when they were up, and listen, as they got the before and after game speeches. I was happy with them when they won, and sad when they lost. I have sat through every kind of weather to watch my team play.

As the coach's wife, I listened to my husband as he ate, slept, and lived the game plans. I could always tell how practice went by looking at his face when he got home at night. He spent so much time away from home that our kids used to ask, "What does Daddy look like?"

At the games, being the coach's wife means that you sit alone or with a very good friend, because they are on the receiving end of the coach's wife shouting and pounding, and always having to wave to her husband on the sidelines while he is coaching.

When the team is winning, everyone is so nice, even complimentary on what a good job your husband is doing. But when the team is behind or losing; watch out; the very same people will bring out their mean and nasty streaks to the surface. At this point, I asked them about their hair problems. If we were losing the game by say 97 points, I, the pure coward, would hide under the bleachers or in the rest room until the game was over.

As the coach's wife, I wanted to be the first person on the field after the game to either greet with a big hug or a consoling pat the man that really made the game.

At home, we replay the entire game. It is then that I heard the ifs and could-have-worked plays. Next morning, the next week's game has already worked itself into our lives.

Coach Powers, my dear husband, decided I needed a job to keep me busy, mainly to keep me from running out on the field and blocking for our sons. Now I think he exaggerated a bit, when he said that I did this 23 times in the first quarter, causing 20 'delay of game' penalties, two off-side penalties and one improper equipment penalty. But, I did know all of the referees by their first name.

The important job that was to be all mine, was to keep the game statistics. This means that first, I had to sit down and stay put. Then write down everything our team did and did not do during the entire game. I asked Hughes if he wanted me to keep track of the band at half time, too. He snorted, "No, smartie. I'm not the band director. I'm the football coach."

After I learned what I was doing, I became so interested in "My Job" and forgot to watch our sons play and Hughes coaching. Keeping the game statistics left me with a permanent side effect of thinking every game of football that I watched; it was My Job to write down the statistics.

The experience I got from my big job made it easier to relive the game for Hughes when he was in the hospital for tests. I knew he was a sick man because he had never before missed attending our sons' football games. I went to the game and took notes all evening for him. Then the next day, during visiting hours, or wherever he happened to be, even in the hall while he was waiting to be X-rayed, I could tell him about the football game that he missed seeing.

Naturally, you're not in excellent condition while they are taking X-rays. But during this particular time, I found Hughes sitting in his wheelchair, drinking a cup of chalk water for the nurse. I could hardly contain myself, to start on the previous night's game rundown. I noticed his face seemed to have a grayish green cast. The nurse said to Hughes, "Be a good boy and drink your little cocktail all gone, gone. Whatever you do, don't lose it because if you do, the doctor won't be able to get a clear picture of your tum-tum and you'll just have to drink another glass full."

I was being patient but anxious to start my resume of the

football game. I pulled up a chair next to his and started to tell him, play by play, the way the game went. I was deep in the fourth quarter and he seemed to be enjoying my replays. When I got to the part of the game where our team almost made a winning touchdown in the final seconds, Hughes did the unpardonable. He lost his chalk cocktail after I finished telling him about our son fumbling the football on the goal line. And I called a quick time out to go find the nurse for my replacement.

During the years that I had three football players and a coach in the house, I wore my football uniform and whistle to work at the beauty salon mainly, because the game nights were Thursday, Friday and Saturday, and whoever wasn't playing those nights had practices.

Sundays, they would play electric football while watching the pro games on TV. The living room was the favorite "after practice" practice place as the boys and Hughes would go over their football plays and discuss the games. It was at this time that I decided that football is 90 percent talk and 10 percent playing time.

Over the years, I found the only way I could get their attention was to get down on the floor and take a 3-point stance and yell, "Hike, supper's ready." This got the best results because that meant training table, and no one wanted to be left out.

My house smelled worse than the locker room of the Miami Dolphins, with the practice jerseys, game uniforms, socks, and jockey shorts which were so strong, that they marched by themselves to the washing machine. My washing machine ran 24 hours a day during football season. The other seasons were a snap because it only ran 17 hours for baseball, 11 hours for basketball and 5 hours for track. Then there were the football helmets, shoulder pads, leg pads, hip pads, mouth pieces, football shoes, three footballs, one set of weights and bench, and one coach's whistle to keep up with. After a while, I felt like a pack rat.

When a problem would arise in our family, regardless the topic, a team meeting was called and the way we measured time was by the different sporting seasons.

My son's idea of staying in shape was to run 40-yard wind sprints to the front gate to get the morning newspaper and then conduct a live scrimmage and whoever ended up on the top of the pile with the sports section in their hand got to read it first that day.

Hobbies enjoyed by the Powers Team that were practiced and played together were "Football" games going on several radio and T.V. stations at the same time. When they got the overactive team spirit, I tried to decide whether I should or shouldn't quit this team for good. Coach Powers said he contributed my problems to having a bad attitude. No dedication and lack of desire.

Being a nervous mother and coach's wife, I thought they couldn't start the game without me, so I was always early. In fact, I was usually in time to watch the men line the field with the down markers.

Pre-game butterflies started the night before the game and didn't fly away until the game was over. Since I had three playing and once coaching, my pre-game butterflies went from pre-game until post-game and finally stayed till the end of the season.

The time my son, Chuck, played football at college; my mother butterflies had so many babies that they ended the season as grandmothers. They seemed to have stayed with me through the previous summer just to make nests to accommodate the next three generations.

During the course of one football season, my record on attendance rose to 26 games. My bleacher cushion disintegrated, the food at the concessions stand was blah, I lost my voice and even my mobility. The last few games I had to be helped to my bleacher seat.

Thinking I had this season finished, by the time I arrived at our house, I found that the family had already started on the next year. It was really a challenge to my boggled mind to know when one season ended and the next one began on the thrill of victory and the agony of defeat.

Tina, our youngest and also the only girl, grew up on the practice field and cut her teeth on the schedules. As a matter of fact, I believe her first words were "touchdown" instead of "Mommy or Daddy." Of course, every place you looked, either at the dairy barn, home or the beauty salon, was a schedule for either football, baseball or track. Basketball had its special place on the front of the refrigerator.

It wouldn't surprise me at all if one day Tina came home from school and said she was playing "Monster Man" on the football team and volunteered me as her backup on the squad.

I have never quite figured out where the word volunteer came from, but I have a sneaking suspicion that maybe my family thought up its meaning.

Volunteer to me means a four letter word in any language – WORK!

Once, my mother said while driving a school bus full of classmates and I on a field trip, "Volunteer work," she yelled over the noise, "is just one of the fringe benefits of being a wife and mother."

I must fess up that when I'm sitting in a club meeting and hear someone announce, "We need a volunteer," suddenly my heart starts pounding, and my palms become clammy. I go into a daze and before I can stop myself with a raised arm waving madly in the air, I shout, "My mother will do it."

Every single time I let it happen, I'll take a sovereign vow to never volunteer for anything ever again.

Unfortunately I'm not the only person in this family that's going through their second childhood. Since the kids are obviously still in their first childhood by their actions, that leaves my husband who is now mid-way into his second. Which means I'm the yo-yo they both volunteer.

Thanks to those rotten kids and their big-mouth father, they're the darndest folks I've ever seen when it comes to volunteering. I never know which one of their projects they'll come up with next to throw me into a depression about. If only I had enough time to go to my group therapy session and discuss their volunteer problem.

My family has always encouraged me on whatever project they had volunteered me for as long as I cook three meals a day, keep the laundry washed, the home spotless, the lawn mowed and weeded, all of the animals fed, plow the west forty and work at the beauty salon. No one could ask for more than to have someone that had volunteered your name and body give you their blessings on their projects, as well as the previous list of priorities.

One of my husband's pet projects that he volunteered nominated, and voted me into was – you guessed it – to be President of the Athletic Booster Club of the school. Hughes chickened out of taking the Pres. Job and instead settled on being a mere board member.

Sometimes a married couple belonging to the same organization can be difficult and entertaining at the same time. We continue the meetings after we return home and often ultimatums are made about him interrupting my meetings without raising his hand first.

The last time it happened, I promised to tape his mouth shut or see him in the divorce court. My husband said, "Not only do I have to hear about the Booster Club for 19 hours a day, I also have to sleep with the President," (but through the course of the Presidency, a little pillow talk with this board member can help get a needed vote.")

One afternoon after coming home from the dairy, Hughes walked through the house which looked a disaster and came to the bedroom, where I had spent most of the day because I had spent most of the day before on a tractor plowing the north forty. I happened to be working on a mock-up of the football program for the year. I was sitting on the floor, in the middle of a pile of cut up papers, gluing my little pieces into place and his comment to me, rather than, "What ya' been doin' all day," was "Holy cow, I'm worried. I think this house has the virus."

I asked, "What?" wondering if maybe the roaches were out again. His answer, "The house looks like it barfed. I better get the shovel from the barn."

The next day my husband came home from the Dairy with a strange look on his face, kind of like the barnyard cat that ate the fat rat looked, and before I could say a word, he mumbled, "I don't know how to tell you this!" That was a familiar phrase, and I knew that I had better head for the couch so I wouldn't fall on the floor.

Hughes stuttered, "You won't have to do the work." I demanded, "Tell me what I won't have to be doing. The last time you said that, and volunteered me, I became Chairman of the Boosters Club Turkey Shoot, and I had never even been to one before in my life, let alone run it."

The news I dreaded to hear was that he had volunteered our house for his Little League baseball team to have a cookout and swim party.

Two things have great power over getting long needed yard work done and things cleaned up. One is a cookout for a group of guests or a hurricane. Ours was the first. Six lawn mowers later, we seemed to have the place looking super nice. Then came the extra guest list.

When our children learned of the party plans they quickly got on the phone and called all of their friends to come spend the weekend with them.

The day of the party, everyone arrived, full of energy and as hungry as bears, read for all of the fun they had been promised. My house looked like the Boardwalk at Daytona Beach during Spring College Break.

The boys were the first in the swimming pool. After a few water fights, they began taking bets as to how many times they could jump off the house roof into the pool without hitting the cement. The games in the other areas started. Bets on the pool table, tobacco spitting contest, and ping pong table, while the stereo blared, rock music that was coming from everywhere. I knew the barn in the front pasture was shaking.

When the "Come and get it" call went out, it was like a feeding frenzy at Sea World. Nothing went to waste. The dogs ate the leftover hot dogs, the horses ate the buns, and the cats finished off the cake.

My husband left the party going in full swing to attend a funeral. The boys who were left helped me, who wasn't supposed to do anything, to clean up the mess. Their idea of helping consisted of licking the picnic table clean, draining the swimming pool and swallowing all of the watermelon seeds.

Each boy said as they were leaving to go home, "Gee, Mrs. Powers I had so much fun, I can't wait till you have the team party next time!"

Foolish me, in a moment of weakness, I had volunteered our house for my husband's next Little League baseball team's party.

"What happened to that vow?" I asked myself. "I blew it again.

Chapter 9

HAIRDRESSER

I am a hairdresser, beautician, hair bender, beauty operator, hair artist, hair stylist, cosmetologist, hair designer, hair sculptor, hair creator, hair specialist, necrocosmetologist and master stylist.

And to my customers I am a psychiatrist, psychologist, psychoanalyst, advisor to the lovelorn, fashion coordinator, tax consultant, marriage counselor, and just plain friend.

To me, a hairdresser is like a doctor; the two professions are similar in many ways. I am called a hair doctor by a lady that walks into the beauty salon every week. The minute she hits the door, she yells, "Is there a doctor in the house?"

You've heard of "Free Advice." Be it medical, legal or cosmetic, you will find people who want it wherever you go. Women, or even men or children, will stop you on the street, or corner you in the grocery store, or grab your arm as you walk in or out of the post office. Their problems, or their friends' problems, are always urgent. Some even ask me about their pet's hair.

The football field is usually where I can be cornered for the longest time. During games I'll be watching the plays, and some female is chattering about, "Why does my hair fall out when I only have sex once a week?" When I'm feeling particularly nice, I listen and try to help with my professional opinion of their sick hair. If they persist, I'll say, "Take two aspirin, and call me at the beauty salon in the morning for an appointment."

People call me day and night, Sundays, Holidays, even on Christmas Eve, for salon appointments. I believe the weirdest time was when Hughes and I were in North Carolina on vacation. A customer called for a color formula that she knew I knew and she needed it because she was on vacation, and another salon in North Carolina was doing her color job, and could I help?

Maybe this is what Mrs. Watson meant in lesson number 5, entitled, "How to Be Famous." People don't seem to realize that you have one appointment book and it is usually in the salon, and a hairdresser's memory, well, that's another story.

This explains how I sometimes get myself in hot water. A person will stop me in the most inappropriate place, like a dark parking lot on a rainy night, and ask for an appointment. I just say, "Come at such and such a time on such and such a day", not really caring at that minute whether I'm booked for that time or not. Sometimes when they appear, I look kinda flabbergasted when there are seven people for that same day and time.

As a hair doctor, I took an oath "to make every woman beautiful." In an emergency, I'll make house calls, whenever and wherever. I have been known to "pick up and deliver" anything to put a smile on a patron's face and a pretty hair style on her head.

They don't even have to be alive. I have worked on dead people's hair for many years in the local funeral parlors. And, so far, I haven't received one single complaint from any of this type of customer. It has been an interesting experience, not only the hair styling work, but how to keep from being caught by the squirrely funeral director, when he chased me around a table in the dark, when the lights went out on a stormy night. I must confess that I have heard some funny jokes and stories told by the funeral directors while in their back rooms.

As proof of my oath, I have all of my State Board of Cosmetology licenses for the last 20 years hanging on the beauty shop walls. I stand tall and proud behind my styling chair, ready to meet any challenge.

Being a practicing Hair Doctor, dedicated to beautifying hair, I cut it, curl it, condition it, rinse it, shape it, bend it, tint it, bleach it, tone it, wash it, wave it, tease it, comb it, straighten it, pin it, and spray it. When all else fails, I talk to it in unkind words, making threats to spit on it or pull it out by the roots (which sometimes disturbs my patrons) if it doesn't behave. If all that doesn't work, being the type of Hair Doctor that I am, I'll look it right on the follicles and say, "What IS your problem today?"

Chapter 10

"GUESS WHAT I SAW AT THE BEAUTY SALON TODAY?"

Of course, a dairy farm wouldn't be that if it didn't have lots of cows. Cows are very curious animals, and I will never forget the two that got out of the pasture and came to visit the beauty salon shortly after we first opened.

Imagine the cow's side of the story. It probably went something like this:

Two Holstein heifers, we'll call them Elsie and Bessie, overheard the milkers in the parlor talking about the new beauty salon in the neighborhood. Not knowing what to expect, Elsie and Bessie thought they had better check this out and see what all the fuss was about. They decided that they wanted to be the first in the herd to visit this new business.

Said Elsie to Bessie: "I'll bet if we drop in at this new beauty parlor, they could squeeze us in."

Bessie was deep in thought trying to figure out what she wanted done with her tail. Finally she came up with the idea that there would be a lot of styling books available inside, and she could find just the right new look for a cow's tail in them.

Elsie was not sure why Bessie was so quiet – maybe she was reconsidering the idea of trying this new place out. With a snide look on her pretty face, she said to Bessie, "That's your problem. You can't make up your mind. Remember the bulls last week?"

Bessie ignored the last comment, still wondering if the curly look would be the best, or if the blown look with wings would be more becoming? Elsie had her mind made up. "All I want is a shampoo and set, with no teasing and lots of pin curls and waves. I want it to last through several milkings."

Bessie looked at her hoofs and figured she was badly in need of a manicure, or a hofficure..."I wonder if they do "Horn Arches," said Elsie. "I need one before I see Ferdinand tonight. Let's look in the window and see how busy they are."

Now, my side of the story: I was busy shampooing a customer, and had two customers under the dryers. In the next room, one of my customers was sitting in a chair next to the window reading a book. Suddenly she let out a 4-alarm scream (I almost dropped my teeth). My first thought was, "Oh no, that darn mouse again."

I quickly ran into the room to find out what was wrong. The lady looked as if she had seen a ghost. She just sat there and kept pointing, trying to tell me that there were two cows looking at her through the window. I told her not to worry, that they wouldn't come into the salon.

Finally calming down, she said, "They are so big!" My reply: "You would be too, if you had four stomachs to feed."

At that minute, I picked up the phone to call my husband at the barn and tell him to come and get his cows. The only sound I got from the phone was a lot of munch, munch noises, and I knew at that time that the phone receiver at the dairy was in the feeding trough again. (The phones at the dairy barn and the beauty salon were on the same party line.) So doing the next best thing, I opened the back door and yelled, "Hughes, come get your cows!"

He came on the run, laughing all the time, and when he finally had the cows under control, he said, "They only wanted to have their hair done." I told him that I wasn't running a special on cow tails today. "And by the way, your phone is off the hook and in the feeding trough again."

After ten years, my patrons now expect the unexpected to happen during their hair appointment.

It seems my beauty salon on the dairy farm is oftentimes, where the beauties meet the beasts as there is even a bullpen in the back yard.

The conversations about the bulls can get very interesting at times.

A bull is the purest form of male chauvinism. All he does all day is eat, sleep, and beller, in a low voice, for someone to bring on the dancing heifers for his show time pleasure.

The pen has four bulls that were never satisfied at the same time, so their love calls went on for hours at a time alone with billows of dust from their hoofs paying the dirt. When my patrons would hear these "love calls" and ask me, "What's that?" I would say, "That's just the old bull."

That was the opening that would bring on some of the funniest comparisons to their husbands you could imagine.

A new customer came in the shop one day to get her hair set, and as I was rolling her hair, "Old Ready Freddie" started his love call from the bull pen. My customer looked like she couldn't believe her ears and asked, "Good gracious, what's that noise?" I told her about Freddy being out back. She said, "I'm a city girl and had never heard anything like that before. Is he sick, hungry or in pain?" I grinned.

"Something like that," and changed the subject.

Sometimes my patrons will even bring their spouse or off-spring along for a tour of the dairy farm. So I guess the beauty salon on the dairy farm has a real entertainment value.

The dairy farm and the beauty parlor being side by side facing a busy four-lane highway is an interesting experience.

Passersby's are forever stopping at the beauty parlor to inform me of the cows' current activities.

The cows that are having a calf seem to be the most prevalent. But my husband being up on the freshing time of his heifers, already knows about it.

If my husband, Hughes, or I don't happen to be at the dairy or the beauty shop, we have people call every Powers in the phone book to give their information to someone.

Here are some typical, random selections from my average dairy-beauty shop cow report log:

-Five people called and three came in, to ask if we had any baby calves for sale. They had seen some in the pasture. I told them to call the dairy. I didn't know how many babies my husband had running around.

-An excited woman ran in and said, "You better get a Vet. One of your cows is having a baby." So I called the dairy to tell Hughes.

-Two women and a man stopped in the shop to report a dead cow laying in the pasture. It turned out she was a sound sleeper.

-Three people called and two stopped in to report that there was a cow stuck in the pond in the pasture. She was just cooling her belly.

-Twenty-nine people called and seventeen came in to ask if we had any bags of cow manure for sale. They had heard from folks that the shop was used as the location to buy the best cow manure around. I told them at one time it was, but now they would have to call the dairy for any requests to buy bags of the good fresh stuff. (This gave me a hair brain idea once, to advertise one free bag of cow manure with each shampoo and set.)

-My kids called to have an argument settled about whose turn it was to get the cows up to the barn for milking time. I told them to call their father, the dairy farmer, and ask him.

-The Sheriff's Department called and asked why there was a traffic jam in front of the dairy. I told them that people were just curious. They were watching a cow have a calf in the Powers' maternity pasture, and there was a rumor out that we planned to charge admission, so they wanted to watch for free.

-Four people called to report that we had a very sick cow in the pasture. She was just old.

-A woman from the Humane Society called to ask about the sick cow. I told her, "Call my husband. That's his cow."

-A very upset woman called and said, "Your cows are eating my garden." It turned out they weren't our cows.

-The Police Department called and said, "Is this Mrs. Powers?" I said, "Yes." The voice said, "Hold a minute." The minute wasted into nine during that time, and everything passed through my mind from one of my children being hurt to goodness only knows. Finally the man came back on the line and said, "Thank you for holding. We had a report that your cows were out in an orange grove and we understand that your husband received a call about an hour ago on this matter." Usually, I ask what the color of the cow is, the number of it, and if it milks. But I was so distraught that I simply forgot everything.

-A man came into the salon not to report, but to casually ask, "Are those your cows standing in the middle of the highway?"

Well, cows on the highway are a 5-alarm emergency that can go off at any time. When it happens, everyone from the dairy and the beauty shop drops whatever they are doing and starts for the highway.

I was busy rolling a customer's hair when the man set off the alarm. Comb in hand and forgetting about my customer, off I went to help get the herd off the highway. It seemed that the whole crew was on their toes this day, as nothing happened to the cows but a little run.

Now it's a different story when the bulls get out. I stay right in the shop and call Hughes and tell him. That's his baby. I refuse to sit in a tree again by trying to help one of the male gender.

The neighboring house on the property houses a milker at the dairy. His hobby is raising chickens, turkeys, ducks, geese, guinea hens, and rabbits, all of which spend a lot of time in the beauty shop yard and deposit there regularly. Add two pregnant cats on the front porch, one tom cat that lives and plays under the shop, two bird dogs that bark all day in the pens in the back yard, two pigs, and an assortment of stray cats and dogs that I can't help but feed, and we have a real "Down on the Farm" Beauty Salon.

On the other hand, if you don't care for those animals, do you want to try for insects, fowl and reptiles that are always around to mix up in a day's sighting? I have green lizards that live in the curtains, a bird nest with baby birds in the chimney that sing for their dinner all day, spiders that make their webs across the front door, a disappearing snake that lives in the oak tree, grasshoppers that live in the plants and eat their share of them and ants that live everywhere. I have three rain frogs that stay in window sills and croak over the sound of the hair dryers, a cricket chirping under the appointment desk, and two plants that seem to grow out of the walls.

And if this isn't enough, my four children come into the shop every five minutes, race through to the store room, open the refrigerator and announce that "there's nothing to eat" and "there's nothing to do." My customers' remark: "Sounds like an instant replay from home."

To make my children instantly disappear, all I have to do is start naming off some fun chores to do – take out the trash, bucket feed the baby calves, wash the inside of the barn, walk instead of ride to get the cows in the barn for milking. The last suggestion is the never fail way to get the children out of the shop and out of my hair.

I ask myself out loud, "What am I doing working in this looney place, and why?" Then I start to sweep down the spider webs from the front door so the customers can get in, chase off the ducks, chickens and other animals, except the chicken that's sitting on eggs on the porch, check and see that the snake if safe in the tree, take my shot gun and shoot to chase all the birds out of the trees so they won't do-do on the customers' cars or their new hair dos, scream "Shut up" 93 times at the dogs, bulls, and guineas in the yards.

Continue screaming while I take the kids to school, come back to the shop and finish the rest of my necessary jobs that mean I will be able to open the doors soon for business. Then my old dream suddenly appears in my mind, and I remember this is the way I know someday, that I will be rich and famous, while I make every woman beautiful. Then I grab the broom again and sweep off a little something that I missed before, and say to myself aloud, "Numbskull, you knew that first day this was not the fancy, sophisticated uptown Beauty Salon. Yeah, but you've got to admit there's never a dull moment around here."

Chapter 11

HOW DO YOU KEEP THEM DOWN ON THE FARM AFTER THEY HAVE SEEN AN UPTOWN BEAUTY SALON

Over the years, I have had an unusual number of hairdressers work for me. They have come and gone after they found I wasn't kidding about my beauty salon not being the average, every day, uptown beauty salon.

The record for the shortest time any employee worked was <u>part</u> of one day. I contribute this to the cows' getting out on the highway three times, having ten calls from my kids, three calls from my mother, two calls from my mother-in-law, seven calls from my husband, a call from my sister-in-law, eleven calls for cow manure and 38 calls from my customers.

I had to leave during a permanent to pick up one kid from the dentist, one from the doctor, one from football practice, one from piano lessons and stop to buy a few groceries.

The capper for this day was the snake and the mouse both came out of their holes at the same time. The girl waited till I got back to the salon, then grabbed her handbag and tore out the door, not looking back. As she jumped into her car, I heard her say, "Fran, you sure weren't kidding when you told me that your salon wasn't the average uptown beauty salon. I'm through."

The two hairdressers that feel at home working in this living TV type soap opera are my sister, Debbie, and my right hand girl, Gloria. They are both "Crazy" Aquarians, and attended the same Beauty School, and they fit right in this "Wacky" beauty salon.

My sister, Debbie, is married and has a dog, and no children. She has a thing about every living, breathing creature, right down to the little mouse that lives in the storage room. She leaves food out for him when we are all at home.

Gloria is a divorcee, the mother of three children, two boys and a girl. She has worked for me for years, so I call her my good right hand. The second day she came to work, she knocked down the spider webs from the front door of the shop, and believe me that is dedication because there is nothing, other than spiders, that she is more afraid of. I knew instantly that between the mouse and the spider webs, these were my kind of people.

I seem to collect special people. My beauty supply salesman, Wally, needs an "Above and Beyond the Call of Duty" award or the "Super Salesman of the Year" award because, for years, he has knocked down spider webs from the front door before he could come in and get my order. I know this must take every ounce of courage he can dig up, because he feels the same about spiders as Gloria does. I always buy something from him, whether I need it or not.

Wally has said on many occasions that all of the beauty salons he calls on, and that has to be hundreds, that mine is "One of a kind." He has also learned that he should not park his car under the trees while he is making his sales call.

Other salesmen aren't as brave as Wally. After three visits to my salon, they decide that they had better phone or write for orders.

All American businesses have rules and regulations for their employees to know and work by. My business is no different. I have posted, in the back storage room, "The Beauty Salon's Employee Rules."

1. Never look better than your customers.
   DO NOT wear make-up or dress up on the job. This will always make your customers look better than you, no matter what you do to them.
2. Leave notes on the front door when you leave the shop for emergencies, shopping or gone fishing. Write the wheres, whens, and whys so the customer will know all of your personal business.
3. Employee parking is always beside the building. Mud puddles and under the tree parking is reserved for customers (when they complain, say that you are sorry about the bird do-do and the wet feet.)
4. Never say no to a money carrying customer that comes into the salon to have her hair set without an appointment, even if you are walking on your knees.
5. Personal phone calls are limited to 8 hours a day.
6. Do not gossip in the beauty salon unless I'm there to hear it.
7. Employees' families and friends may visit on the job between the hours of 8:30 a.m. and 5:00 p.m., Monday through Saturday.
8. Always write personal messages on the appointment book.
9. If water goes off, call Hughes at the dairy.
10. Plumbing and hot water heater problems, call Granddaddy Powers.

11. Animals and children problems, call Fran. Cow out on the highway, call the dairy first, then go out and help get them rounded up.
12. Never, I repeat, never, open the beauty shop at night without first kicking and screaming to announce your arrival. This is for your safety. Everything or one should be well hid before your body crosses the threshold.

Debbie is our night person. This explains why she sleeps with her head in the shampoo bowl during the day, and wakes up when the sun goes down. Her hobbies start late in the evening and many a time, after I have been asleep for hours and am in the middle of a fantastic dream, my phone will ring and it will be Debbie.

Hughes usually answers the phone during the night, because that is the time that the cows like to start their meandering out of the pasture and someone always calls and lets him know about his roving cows. But this time, he handed the phone to me and said, "It's Debbie."

I said, "Hello," while I yawned.

"Frannie, I'm sorry to call you so late, but I have a problem." Before she could get the rest of the sentence finished, my heart stopped. "I'm in the beauty shop."

I couldn't figure out whose hair she was doing at 2:30 a.m., so I asked her, "What or whose hair is so important that you would be working now?"

She said, "Oh, I'm not doing anyone's hair, I just finished weeding all of the flower beds and cleaned the shop and now I can't decide what color paint to use. Can you come down and help me decide?"

I told her, "Its 2:30 in the morning. You just interrupted a fantastic dream and I want to get back to it. You have good taste so whatever color you decide on will be okay with me. Goodnight!"

Thinking I had dreamed all of the conversation of the night before, when I got to the beauty shop in the morning, I was greeted with a perfectly groomed yard, a clean beautiful beauty salon, and freshly painted rust colored shutters. Debbie had struck again and was home sleeping, while I worked in the beautifully cleaned beauty shop alone.

Not only is Gloria my right hand girl, she is also right handed. This has made it much easier in this small beauty salon, because left handed and right handed hairdressers, working side by side, always get in each other's way.

We have a lot in common. The reasons are so similar, when it comes to not working at times. We are sick, our kids are sick, our animals are sick, or our cars won't start.

Gloria, Debbie and I are like hairdressers the world over. We all have a favorite comb and brush to use. We feel the secret to our great success is the worn out, toothless, metal teasing comb. Being the fun loving girls that we are, we hide it from each other, or fight over whose turn it is to use it.

Our customers, on different occasions, have brought us new combs to use on their hair. We say, "thank you," and then hide the new combs out in the bullpen in the back yard. When a new customer asks us why we use that ugly old toothless teasing comb, we quickly tell them that we can't work with any other comb. It's like a magic wand and works all the miracles.

When the favorite toothless teasing comb comes up missing, everyone is frantic. Even with drawers full of other combs, all work stops and the "Missing Comb Alarm" is sounded. We start an inch by inch search of our customers, their cars in the parking lot, the pasture and the bull pen. We call the dairy barn and my mother-in-law's house to see if the comb is hiding over there. The next call goes to the Sheriff's Department to see if there have been any reports of the missing metal toothless comb.

One frantic week the metal toothless teasing comb came up missing and it couldn't be found anywhere. The family was busy with the county fair as well as all the other activities that were going on, but the missing comb was never out of our minds.

The whole family had a date to go to the fair and see the livestock auction and judging, which our son, Chuck, had a part in. He had his entry all fattened up, cleaned and "combed" and ready for judging.

Last minute touch ups brought the lost metal teasing comb and the missing blow dryer to the surface in the livestock barn. The sight of that comb got Debbie, Gloria and I to our feet in the stands. There stood Chuck, tall and proud, combing the snarls out of his steer's tail. It only took 1-2-3 and we were out of our seats, down with the animals, to get our hot little hands on the stray comb. We were then assured that the comb was a magic wand because Chuck's entry had won first prize. Looking around the cattle barn we also found the missing brush and the near full can of hair spray that he had been using.

I tell my mother how lucky she is to have two daughters that are hairdressers, two daughters that are secretaries, grandmother to seven mean kids, 16 pets and be the bookkeeper of the beauty salon.

We have a quick and easy bookkeeping system. I let her read all of my bills, and then we talk about them over the phone while I'm working. During income tax time, my mother and I stay on the phone for hours on end, and days and days. My regular customers, having gone through this time of year before, say, "How's your mother, tell her hello for me." Or, "How's your mother's plants growing?"

When mother comes to the beauty salon for her weekly hair appointment, we hold a mini family reunion in the beauty shop. Usually attending are mother, sister Debbie, Mother Powers, my sister-in-law Doris, my husband's Aunt Mabel, sister Charlotte, my kids (who keep running in and out), my daddy, when he needs a haircut, my husband (to see what's going on) maybe mother's poodle, Gloria, and of course, our customers.

The conversations at these beauty shop reunions cover what all has been happening since the last week's reunion, who's sick, with what and why. Then the ones that aren't there are discussed until the entire family tree has been covered.

My mother always leaves the shop saying, "How do you stand it?"

I really can't stand it, but she is referring about everyone trying to talk at the same time and being drowned out by the noise from the hair dryers.

I can always tell when the other hairdressers in town are on vacation or sick leave. Sometimes, their customers come to my beauty salon for an appointment until their operators are back to work. At these times, Gloria, Debbie and I get caught up to date on the experiences of the operators at the other salons. The rest of the time, we get second hand information from our customers about their friends' hairdressers. All this saves visiting between hairdressers, as we know what is happening in each other's lives.

One day, after I finished giving Zenda's customer a permanent wave, I know how many friends Zenda's five children had, her dog's favorite brand of dog yummies, and what Zenda's first night on her honeymoon was like.

While rolling her hair, I listened to one of Mr. Bob's customers tell about the extra services she received as his customer. Seems like good old Mr. Bob gives special conditioning treatments in the backroom of his salon. No wonder he has a reputation as the busiest and fastest hairdresser in town.

As a hairdresser, salon owner, zoo keeper, wife of a dairy farming ex-coach, mother of four (my mother will bake it) kids, Booster

Club President, (that holds pep rallies in the library), I have learned to expect the unexpected problems that happen regularly.

I always tell Debbie and Gloria to call me at home if they have a problem at the shop on my day off. Really this means, "Do not call me unless you are planning to die under the shampoo bowl with the beauty shop full of unfinished paying customers." When I hear the voice of one of them on the phone, my heart stops for a full minute.

Here I was, enjoying a nice restful day at home with my four children, happy over the fact that I had found the ringing noise that had been bugging me for the last few hours. It was the telephone hidden in the over, again.

Having four telephone hungry children that hide the phone from each other, made me go into my "Don't hide the telephone lecture." The first chapter covered: "Do not hide the phone in the oven, rabbit pen, laundry hamper, under the beds, in dresser drawers, in the attic, in the refrigerator, in the washer or dryer, under the water heater, the glove compartment of the car or cattle truck, in the linen closet or their closets, or god forbid, the swimming pool."

I was ready to start on chapter #2, "What will happen to you if you hide the phone one more time and I catch you..." Suddenly the phone rang, the children all jumped, as I was holding it in front of their noses to get my point across to them during my lecture.

I answered the phone very calm, saying, "Hello."

Gloria's voice was on the other end. My heart instantly stopped beating for a full minute, while I listened to Gloria describe the problem at the beauty salon. It seems that a cow was standing in the septic tank, eating grass off of the top while cooling her feet.

At this point, my stomach rose back to its normal position. She went on to tell me that there were a dozen customers in the shop and five of them needed to use the restroom, and "Mr. John" was running all over the floor.

I asked her if she had called Granddaddy Powers; he's listed under "Plumbing Problems." She said she had already called him. "Have you gone out and tried to remove the cow from the septic tank?"

Silence was the only reply I got. I went on talking, "Now, Gloria, I know that you are afraid of spiders and cows, but this one time, please go outside and talk to the cow."

She finally agreed she would try. I told her to call me back if she needed help.

When I hung up, the kids wanted to know what the latest shop problem was because they wanted a good laugh. I told them it was not a laughing matter when you have a shop full of women and Mr. John goes on strike.

Gloria said that she had to redo a lady's hair because she had cried all over herself while waiting so long for Mr. John to get back to work.

While waiting for Gloria to call back, I listened to my daughter, Tina's, latest recording of yesterday's argument with her brother. Her hobby is taping every word that is said or barked, with her portable tape recorder. She has it with her at all times, always read to set it off and running.

After the tape was finished playing she asked, "Do you want to hear it again?" I told her, "No. Three times would be just too much to take. Remember, I heard the original argument yesterday."

I kept worrying about the cow in the septic tank at the beauty shop, and I decided that since I was a distant relative to that cow by marriage, I might be able to talk it out of the septic tank.

I was heading for the door when the phone rang. "Hello," I said. "Fran," (my heart stopped again). It was Gloria. "Granddaddy has located the plumbing problem. It wasn't the cow in the septic tank that was causing the trouble," she reported. "Then what caused the problem?"

Gloria replied that someone had flushed an old used wig down Mr. John and he choked. "Granddaddy said it sure gave him a scare when he pulled out the wet wig. He said he first thought that we had gotten mad at one of our customers and scalped her."

I'm sure the Beauty Shop problem calls during my days off will continue until I retire, or I go wacko and I'm forced to retire early to a funny farm.

Phone rings. I scream, "Hello." "Frannie," (my heart stops; its Debbie's voice) "I hate to bother you on your day off but I have a problem." "What now?" "There's a customer here demanding money for a car wash. She parked her shiny new white car under the trees while she got her hair styled and the birds used it for target practice and she's really mad about it." Debbie's voice was down to a mere whisper.

I started, "You tell her that the bird do-do is an act of nature."

On one of my days off, I noticed half way through the day that I hadn't had a report from the beauty shop and I thought maybe today is the day that I'm going to not have any trouble calls.

My day went along quite ordinary; the phone rang, but the messages were for my husband and the kids. I wrote down everything so I would get the messages right.

Hughes list of calls was: two feed salesmen called. Mrs. Jones called and wants to buy 300 fence posts. Tommy called and wants to borrow the tractor. The Sheriff's Department called three times and said our cows were out in a neighbor's garden. Five calls from the dairy: 1- you have a sick cow laying down in the feed trough; 2- the uniform delivery man wants his check; 3- the milk tank cooling motor burned up; 4- Steve called to borrow your truck; 5- how many calves do you have to sell?

The vet called to give you a report on the sick cows. Your mother, your sister, your father and your brother called and said for you to call them back. Mrs. Brown called for her son, who wanted to know what time football practice was today. I told her that you were retired. Mrs. Jackson called to buy a pickup truck load of cow manure delivered.

The children's calls: Tell them all to return calls to all their frantic friends.

My mother called and asked me who had been talking on the phone because it had been busy for the last four hours. Mother and I talked for almost two hours, and after I hung up, I thought to myself, "This is great! No problem telephone calls from the shop this morning."

At that moment, the phone rang again, and I answered, "Hello."

"Fran," (my heart stopped beating) "we have run out of towels and the hot water heater is acting up again." Gloria kept on, "There's a lady stuck in the ditch with her truck blocking traffic."

No doubt, my day was complete.

A psychiatrist would have a field day with my family's problems. They must suffer from deep emotional insecurity or lost personality symptoms, or better yet, losing-people symptoms. They are forever asking where every member of the family is if they aren't right under their noses.

"Where's dad?" "Where's Mom?" "Where's David?" "Where's Chuck or Marshall?" (I ask this a lot), or 'Where's Tina?" Sounds like a roll call at camp. But it doesn't stop at home. It goes on to the dairy, and the beauty salon, by telephone.

I was having one of those days, answering the telephone 36 times between shampoos and sets, telling each caller, "No, Gloria isn't here. It's her day off."

While shampooing my last customer's hair, I could hear the faint ringing of the telephone that I had hidden in the back room in the dirty towel bin after I had had my last call. The darn thing kept on ringing and ringing. Finally, I decided it may be an important call. Leaving my lady's head in the shampoo bowl, I went running into the back room and started pulling the dirty towels out of the dirty towel bin, just to find the telephone so I could answer it. (A gym locker room smells like roses compared to a week's supply of used beauty shop towels). I finally found the telephone, grabbed the receiver, trying to catch my breath after standing upside down in the towel bin, and the voice on the other end said, "French Toast, where's Dad?"

    Marshall had gotten through to me, again.

Chapter 12

OUT YONDER IN THE COW PASTURE

I am often asked by beauty customers, "Where do you live?" They can see that it's not in the beauty shop. I usually answer while I point, "In the cow pasture."

There's a great advantage living "way out back in the pasture" because when all my problems get the best of me, I just run like the dickens out in the middle of the pasture and scream my lungs out. It really works wonders. There the only ones that hear me are the cows, who graze most of the day.

During summer vacation, when the kids are home from school all the time and play the let's drive mother nutsy game, I wear a path from the house to the pasture and sometimes the cows casually look up and, I can almost hear them say, "Oh no. Here she comes again."

The disadvantage of living out yonder in the cow pasture is having to give my friends directions when they visit. My house can't be seen when the corn field is "as high as an elephant's eye" so they call for complete information before starting up the lane.

Patty called and asked, "Fran, I was going to come over for a little visit. Is the front gate opened or locked? I just hate to get out of my car, open the gate, get back into my car, drive through, get out of my car and close the gate, get back in my car and drive to the house, especially, twice." I tell her, "Pat, you're in luck. The gate is open. Come on over."

Alice called: "Fran, if you're not busy, I'll come over and have a cup of coffee, but first I want to know where the bull is. Is he in the pasture by the gate, or just where? You know I have a red car and he's not too fond of it." I tell Alice, "Come on over. The bull is "on duty" at the dairy barn today."

One of the most frequent complaints is from Trail. She'll call to see if the cows are in the pasture next to the gate. She called one day, and I told her to come on, but when she got through the gate and up the lane a ways, there were the cows, laying in the road, and they wouldn't move. She honked her horn and yelled at them and they just laid there and chewed their cuds, as if to say, "Don't bother us now. We're busy making milk." By the time she got up to the house, 25 minutes had elapsed. I had begun to believe that she wasn't coming.

The phone rang, and I heard Rita's voice saying, "Fran, I thought I would come and visit if your driveway is in the same place. Last time it rained, your driveway disappeared and I got stuck. Remember, the last time I came, your son Chuck had to pull me and the car out with his tractor?" I said, "Rita, we have a new driveway since last night's rain. Turn off the highway and stay on the old dirt road, then take a sharp right by the telephone pole, and then another right straight through the hole in the barb-wire fence."

Mary called: "Fran, if that mean black dog of yours is tied up, I'll come over for a while, but the last time, I thought I was going to be his dinner." I said, "Come on, Mary. You won't have to worry today because he has already eaten two motorcycle helmets that belonged to my kid's friends."

No wonder, most of my friends are also my beauty shop customers. The beauty salon is easier to get to and we can visit while I style their hair, relax under the dryers and have a cup of coffee. They listen to all of this hairdresser's problems, and then pay me for their hairdo. What better friends could a hairdresser ask for?

But then again, I still wouldn't trade living on the cows' side of the fence with anyone. That is, until July came and it was halfway through school vacation time.

I knew that the kids had won their game and I was going "nutsy" because I had already worn a path into the pasture from walking, or sometimes running, to the pasture to scream. My customers, knowing how bad my nerves were, got together and hired a retired college demonstrator to walk back and forth in front of the beauty shop carrying a sign that said, "Fran's in one of her moods." That kinds of warns late customers and no-appointment customers, that "all is not well."

I called my mother to beg for help. "Mother, this is your number two child, and I need your help. Your grandchildren are driving me up the wall."

Mother said, "Have you been wearing Hughes' big, black belt around your neck?" I told her that I had been wearing it and singing nursery rhymes.

She knew that something must be done, but what? "How can I help?" she questioned.

"Mother, I beg you, please, just this one time, can the children come to visit you for 25 minutes and give me a rest? I'll even pack them a lunch."

"Number two child, you know that I have my hands full with

your baby sister."

This stopped me cold. "Mother, I know, but my baby sister is 20 years old!"

Springtime the following year, one Monday morning, my first customer in the beauty salon started to tell me about her perfect children and how she couldn't wait for summer vacation to begin, and all the plans she had ready for them.

Now, that patron was an over active Super Mom type. She went everywhere and did everything with her perfect children. When she insisted on telling me all of her plans for the summer, she added, "I just know that you can't wait for school to be out this year, too."

I told her that I started counting the days until school started again before the last bell rang on the last day of school.

From that day forward, we talked about the weather or anything but children when she had her appointment with this "nutsy" hairdresser.

Chapter 13

WILL THE REAL TROUBLEMAKER PLEASE STAND UP?

"Oh nuts, not another crisis in the beauty salon," bellowed my husband's voice over the telephone after I had called the dairy barn to confront him with our mutual problem of the moment.

No matter how you say it, a beauty parlor and a milking parlor without water can make for a dirty problem.

The water system for the barn, beauty salon, and my neighbor's house, consists of one well with a very unpredictable pump that's located near the dairy's barn. Looking back over the years, I'll never forget the first of many times the cantankerous son-of-a-gun went on the fritz.

A few days after I opened the beauty shop for business, it happened. I was working on a customer, Mrs. Ida Mae Peabody, who was an 87 year old retired school teacher from Piney Woods, Georgia. From the look and feel of Ida Mae's head, she had used two handfuls plus half a fist, just for good measure of greasy kid's stuff on her hair.

I poured blots and globs of shampoo on her hair and finally worked up a rich, foamy lather on her head. When I turned on the faucets in the sink to rinse the shampoo out of her hair, nothing came out of the sprayer hose. Not even one little drop of water dribbled out. "Oh, spit," I said angrily, shaking the daylights out of the dry-as-a-bone shampoo sprayer hose with both hands.

Just then I thought my deodorant wasn't working by the way Mrs. Peabody kept staring up at me from the shampoo bowl. While I went to the phone and frantically dialed my husband's number to tell him my water was off, I left Mrs. Peabody's head hanging in the sink as soap bubbles floated around in the air from her hair.

A man answered the phone at the barn and said, rather bored, "Hang on lady. I'll go find him."

Water, water everywhere, but not a drop to rinse with, as visions of the cow pond came to my mind, while I waited for my husband to come and answer the phone.

I glanced at the soapy-headed woman in the sink, who looked like the Lawrence Welk bubble machine just then, and said to her, "Don't worry, it's only a minor problem. I'm sure my husband will have the water back on in a few minutes. Just hang in there, Mrs. Peabody."

With a shrug, she remarked, "So this is what I get for coming to this neck of the woods and your hole in the wall beauty parlor to get my hair done."

At that moment, Mrs. Peabody nodded her head and more bubbles filled the room. By that time, I was up to my eyeballs in shampoo bubbles.

Where is that man when I need him the most, I thought, working myself up into a tizzy as I held the telephone receiver to my numb ear. The 20-foot phone cord made a neat jump rope. But I soon pooped out from jumping it too fast.

I stood there on one foot and then on the other and looked across the room at my reflection in the mirror and said, "Mirror, mirror on the wall, who's the most beautiful of them all... Me of course," I admitted with a sigh. "Why fight it. I'm definitely an over-the-fence sex symbol," sticking my tongue out at the mirror's reflection and yanking a grey hair out of my head, knowing full well that seven more would grow back in its place.

"Were you talking to me, honey?" asked Mrs. Peabody.

"No," I said. And watched the mirror in horror as Mrs. Peabody's shampoo bubbles busted, then slowly, one by one, dried on her head.

Finally, I heard my husband's voice on the phone. "What's the matter now?" he asked irritably.

I decided to go for it and yelled into the receiver in a very unladylike manner, "The water is off in the beauty parlor. I can't rinse the shampoo out of my customer's hair without running water, and you better turn my water back on."

"Right on, girlie!" shouted Mrs. Peabody, pounding the arms of the styling chair with her fists. "That's the way to tell 'em. Dog gone, this sure beats the heck out of watching Family Feud on T.V."

I did my best. Then realized, as I caught my breath I had ranted and raved and carried on about the beauty salon's problem, that my husband hadn't uttered a single peep. He had only made snorting noises that resembled an enraged bull into the phone receiver.

"Are you finished?" he asked, through clenched teeth. I yelled, "You bet your rubber boots I'm finished," and that shook the barn.

Hughes cleared his throat, took a deep breath, and then told me in his megaphone voice, which I could hear without a telephone line between us since his dairy barn is located only a stone's throw way from my beauty parlor.

No doubt about it, I knew where he was coming from just then as I held the phone receiver at arm's length and listened to my husband, in his good ole' southern drawl. "Let me tell you about my problems, Missus. If you think you have one," he said, "right this minute I have 453 dirty-bagged cows that need to be milked standing on a muddy ramp, and the wires on the water pump motor just burnt up so, you'll have to just set on it until I can fix the old sumbitch."

When I heard the odds, 453 to 1, I hung up the phone, pulled up a chair to set my buns on and went back to watching the rest of my customer's shampoo bubbles dry on her head.

"Mrs. Peabody," I sighed, "What's a nice girl like me doing working in a joint like this?"

Mrs. Peabody raised her soapy head out of the shampoo bowl, pointed a crooked finger my way and said, "Sugar pie, remember Scarlett O-Hara's immortal words, 'Tomorrow is another day'."

"Feedle de, who cares? I'll think about that later," I sighed. Then thought, frankly right now, I don't give a darn, as we continued to wait for the familiar sound of the drip, drip of water in the shampoo bowl to return.

A couple of suns and moons passed by and a few weeds grew in the garden before the cantankerous son of a gun pulled its nasty act again. But this time, Gloria was the one in the beauty shop without water to use on her patron's hair.

At the time, I was home and was busy as a bee working in the garden, picking vegetables, between canning and freezing them. My kitchen looked similar to a roadside vegetable stand after a tornado hit it, what with the stacks of canning jars and lids, freezer bags and vegetable peelings scattered all over the place.

The phone rang and when I answered it, then heard Gloria's voice, my heart stopped beating as I knew there was a problem at the beauty shop. I thought about hanging up and hiding my body under the mess in the kitchen so I wouldn't have to leave the over ripe vegetables, pressure cooker and freezer guide book to go to the beauty salon. Meanwhile, I listened as Gloria excitedly explained that there was no water to rinse Mrs. Lulu Flamingo's permanent wave solution out of her hair.

Now, if one problem wasn't enough, it so happened that Mrs. Flamingo was the preacher's wife from over in the next town and her hair was over curling.

Well, just for the record, any beautician knows that when a permanent needs turned off, you better run to the nearest water. Just then, the only thing that came to my mind was that Mr. John in the shop had gallons of water that Gloria could use to rinse her patron's hair. After all, this was an emergency and I old Gloria the procedures to follow.

I waited anxiously for Gloria to call back to tell me how the rescue of Mrs. Flamingo's permanent turned out with Mr. John's assistance.

Finally, Gloria called and, with a sigh of relief, said Lulu told her, "It must have been the country water because this was the best permanent she had ever had." Unbeknown to me at the time, I wasn't the only salon owner with water problems. The rest, as they say, is history.

One afternoon on a typical work day, Gloria, Debbie and I were hard at work on our patrons' hair. I was shampooing Mrs. Smith, while munching a Girl Scout cookie. We had sold 57 boxes of cookies that day and were busily finishing off the last box. All of the customers had eaten cookies under the hair dryers and the crumbs were ankle deep in the shop.

The phone rang for the 194th time; Gloria answered it and then said, "Fran, Mr. Tim wants to talk to you."

"Tell him just a minute," as I was swallowing the cookie, then washed the shampoo off my hands and left Mrs. Smith to relax in the sink while I talked on the phone.

Mr. Tim is a fellow hairdresser friend and down the road a piece neighbor, and the owner of Mr. Tim's Uptown Styling Salon. We borrow hair products from each other like housewives borrow laundry soap or sugar. It seems we're forever running out of something important we need for our customer's hair. Mr. Tim and I keep the phone lines busy with our constant borrowing; however, we never ask to borrow each other's customers.

I knew something terrible was wrong when I said, "Hello," and he didn't laugh and say, "Is this Fran's Beauty Supply Company?" or whisper into the receiver, "Birdie, the State Board Inspector is in town and headed your way." That comment from him always guaranteed a shiny and sparkling clean as a pin beauty salon in record breaking time.

"Someone turned my water off," said Mr. Tim, with hysteria in his voice. "I can't seem to get a handle on my plumbing problem. I called the plumber and his answering service said he was out playing golf. I need to borrow your water. There's three ladies with permanent waves, two with hair tints, and five with shampoo on their heads, that need rinsing off."

I quickly hung up the phone to alert Debbie and Gloria to clear the decks, as Mr. Tim was coming in with his beauty shop patrons for a water stop.

'Hurry, ladies," shouted Mr. Tim, as he unloaded his troupe from the van and herded them through the door. One after another, Mr. Tim rinsed his customers' heads with water as my patrons stood and watched with wicked grins on their faces. Over the shampoo bowl I said softly to Mr. Tim, "You know, we gotta stop meeting like this." He only rolled his eyes around kept on mumbling, "My reputation will be ruined."

Mr. Tim's customers and mine put on a staring match. My ladies acted as if his patrons were strangers who had dropped in for supper uninvited.

"My, my," said one of Mr. Tim's patrons, as she frantically fanned her face with her hands, "How do you people stand the aroma of the dairy farm in here?" I looked at the woman who then fanned herself with the shampoo cape, and thought, without a doubt, that woman's a super wacko.

As every pair of eyes in the beauty shop stared at her, "Pardon me, Ma'am," I said to the woman, handing her a piece of bathroom tissue, "You stepped where the dog had been. You wanta wipe it off your shoes?"

Finally Mr. Tim and the giggling gang of dripping wet heads left for the luxuries of his uptown salon.

While chewing on a piece of hay, I said to them without smiling, "Y'all come back to see us, you heah?"

Before the dust from Mr. Tim's van settled back into the potholes and ruts in the parking lot, the water went off in my beauty shop.

At that moment, my husband's muffled roar of "Aw shucks" echoed across the farm. His voice came from the bottom of the milk tank that he just happened to be washing at the dairy's barn.

THE MOODY OLD DEVIL GOES ON STRIKE

Having no water isn't much more frustrating than not having any HOT water. That wasn't uncommon at the Beauty Salon. Our water heater had reached the ripe old age of 45 years. And, while retirement wasn't on its agenda, it sure was tired.

I remember one particular freezing day when I had a full appointment book and a salon full of dirty headed patrons. The "Old

Moody Devil" decided that was the day to go on strike again.

"Not today of all days," thought I as I tottered into the back room. Opening the closet door where "the culprit of the day" lived, I started a full-fledged conversation with it in my most calm, serene voice.

"You're such a striking hot water heater; you wouldn't do this to me today, would you? Couldn't you make just a little hot water for Gloria and me?

I called to Gloria to check the shampoo bowl in the other room and she came up with a "No, not yet."

Now I knew that I had to get to my "get down to business" talk. So in a very apologetic tone, I looked right in the heating element and said, "Okay, I'm sorry I called you the "Moody Old Devil" and I promise that I will never do it again, if you'll just behave yourself and make us some hot water. Besides, if you don't work in this establishment, you don't get paid." Hoping this walk had done the trick, I called to Gloria to see how my pep talk had worked. "Nope, no hot water yet," was the reply.

My temper began to flare and my blood pressure rose to its ultimate high. I began, "Now listen here, you. If you don't start making hot water right now, I'll hit you and kick you in your big metal sides."

Nothing I said seemed to change its mind. He even saw more patrons coming into the beauty salon that were depending on him, but no deal; he was on strike.

Of course he figured that he could go on unemployment if he got fired, so he was testing me, little did he realize that there was an alternative. He could sit in his closet and sulk, figuring that he had the upper hand this day. But little did he know that I had called workers at the dairy barn next door to borrow hot water to wash all of the dirty heads that he had disappointed.

We carried hot water in 10-gallon milk cans, most of the afternoon. Gloria and I were not strangers to inconvenience but this was ridiculous, just because of the Moody Old Devil. Gloria and I fulfilled our oath of making all women beautiful, regardless of the obstacles.

That year, I received a most special birthday present, one that made Gloria and me and our patrons very happy. My special birthday present was delivered to the beauty salon, wrapped in a beautiful package, big ribbon on the top, with a card that said, "Happy Birthday, Fran. Love, Granddaddy and Mother Powers."

After I opened it, I cried, because it was just what I wanted. It was the right size and the right color and I couldn't wait to use it. My patrons, as well as Gloria and I, enjoyed it from the beginning. It was a heating element for the Moody Old Devil. Then I realized that he had really been sick and all he needed was this new transplant, because the ornery cuss hasn't let me down since.

Chapter 14
THOSE MUDDY LITTLE RASCALS

If into every life some rain must fall, then no wonder folks around these parts say, "Rain, rain go away. Come again another day," when they have to wade through the mud puddles in the parking lot to get to my Beauty shop.

And, if folks are like me, their umbrella is in the trunk of the car when they need it.

Take our cows. They don't worry about umbrellas or wet feet. They simply turn their tails to the wind and enjoy the shower until the boss cow decides she's had enough of the heavenly water and heads for the shelter of a nice dry barn. Then the others will tag-a-long in her hoof prints.

To me a rainstorm means lightning, mud and having a herd of kids inside the beauty shop or house. When the raindrops fall, my children begin to beg and nag to play in the rain, so they can have fun making delicious mud pies. Then they dare me to taste the gross looking stuff.

When I'm home and there is a thunder storm with lightning flashing and cracking from the sky, I do what any normal true blue frightened soul does. I run to a closet and hide in the dark or crawl under the bed and cover my head with a pillow until it passes over.

But, on the other hand, at work I do the next best thing. I sit cross-legged in the center of the dryer room floor and pray.

The other day, how can I ever forget it, during a thunderstorm, the lightning hit the transformer at the dairy. This gave the cows in the milking parlor a real thrill of an electric shock. When the red fireball of lightning flashed and the sonic boom of the thunder followed, it sure scared the dad-burned stuff'in out of me, as each hair on my head stood straight up on end. Suddenly, the lights went off in the beauty shop and I stood combing a customer's hair in the dark.

A lady who had been sitting under the dryer in the next room was now squatted on the floor. When I looked at her, I knew instantly that we shared the same respect for lightning. I joined her on the floor as the wind rocked the building and it continued to pour cats, dogs, and tadpoles. I thought, "This is definitely not a farmer's kind of rain. I just hope this beauty shop will float. Whoever's doin' their rain dance can quit now."

The woman dipped her snuff as we sat on the floor talking. Then we did a yoga exercise or two in the dark. It made me dizzy and gave me a pain in my neck, so we stopped. Finally I thought what a shame we didn't have a deck of cards or jacks or even some marbles to play during my recess time from working.

Just then, I went to the window to check on the storm's progress and shouted, "Where's the idiot that parked their motorcycle on the front porch?" At that moment, in walked Elroy, wearing a baseball cap, motorcycle boots and outfitted in the preppy look, and soaked through the bones. I said, "Oh, c'mon Elroy, that's a cop out. Don't you want to get stuck in the mud puddles like everyone else when it rains?"

"My horn doesn't blow and I didn't want to chance it," Elroy said, shaking water onto the carpet like a wet hound dog. "I read your sign out front, 'Honk if you need a tractor.' How much do you charge for that service?"

I said with a shrug, "There's no extra charge if a customer's vehicle gets stuck in the parking lot, or falls into the ditch and needs to be pulled out with the tractor."

Elroy said grinning, "I want to make an appointment for a haircut next week before my date with a real foxy chick who goes by the C.B. handle of Buffy."

He stopped talking, sniffed the air, and then asked, "What's that horrible odor I smell? It must be coming from the dairy farm when it rains."

I said, holding my nose, "That's a wet skunk under the beauty shop."

Suddenly I heard a car horn honking loudly out front, which meant the next customer had got their car stuck past the fenders in the parking lot. I located the telephone and called Hughes, "Another one bites the mud. Hurry, bring the tractor!"

I looked out the window as the woman opened her car door, then pulled off her shoes and rolled up her pants legs and started to swim through the mud puddles to the beauty shop.

Elroy said, as he opened the door to leave, "The good Lord willing and the mud puddles in the parking lot don't rise; I'll see you next week for my hair appointment at the same time."

I searched through the dark beauty shop for a life jacket. If those muddy little rascals out there were ten feet deep and rising, I planned to be ready for them when they came under the door.

Chapter 15

POTPOURRI OF COUNTRY STUFF, AND THINGS

My beauty salon and our family's dairy farm both seem to be bureaus for vital information. It seems that people are always stopping to get answers to questions ranging from A to Z.

Regardless of the hour, they will dial up family's hot line numbers. If they can't reach any of our clan by phone, then they hop in a vehicle and drive to our farm to inquire in person about their needed information. So, on our dairy farm or in my beauty salon if you ask it, we'll answer it or find someone who can.

Then there are some folks who don't want anything in particular. They'll just stop by to sit a spell and chat about all of the news of the countryside as they pass the time of day with us. It seems ours is still the place to go when there's nothing to do.

I reckon the beauty shop and the dairy farm attract more people to them than flies to honey.

And speaking of honey and other unusual items found in a country store, my beauty salon, oftentimes resembles the inside of a medicine man's wagon with wares of every shape and description for sale.

In my beauty salon, if you want it, we got it. Or, maybe you forgot it and we'll locate it in the lost and found department.

My customers describe the beauty shop as the best country store they have ever shopped in. Folks, hereabouts, can't wait to find out what the next shipment of merchandise might contain.

The other day, I got a wild hair and made a list of the stock that's for sale.

THE COUNTRY STORE BEAUTY SHOP INVENTORY LIST:
1. Professional beauty and hair care products (for those who care to use only the very best, of course.)
2. Girl Scout Cookies for the troop, peanut butter candy for the bank, chocolate mints for the PTA, cheese and sausage for the FFA, homemade bread, brownies, cakes and pies for the church bake sale, pecan log candy for the FHA (for anyone who has a sweet tooth, or is just plain hungry.)
3. Thirteen house plants in hanging containers, inside the shop.

And, on the front porch, sixty-seven yard shrubs and flowers in tin cans, courtesy of my mother's green house and plant nursery (for folks who don't have a green thumb.)

4. A cord of firewood, stacked under the oak tree in the yard, with a sign nailed on the tree that reads, "Firewood 4 Sale, U-Load."
5. Pens, pencils, stationary, calendars, magazine subscriptions. The school's colors and insignia on bumper stickers; baseball hats, hankies, banners and spirit pins. One can even buy an ad in the football program, raffle tickets, or a reserve seat pass for the football season. Then there are tickets for upcoming events, plus stuffed animals and knitted booties, candles and greeting cards (these latter items are for the early or late Christmas shoppers.)
6. Inside the shop there is enough produce from out of my garden to fill a large vegetable stand – all but the fresh green onions, they're on the back porch. (I've found the smell of hair spray and onions don't mix well together.)
7. For the people who want something for nothing and will take anything we give away, there are empty plastic bottles and a bag of hair clippings. Old newspapers, magazines and campaign literature, oranges and grapefruit from the trees in the yard, a cutting off my favorite plant, plus tour maps of the dairy farm with an X on them that marks the spot to dig for humongous fishing worms.

My country store beauty shop is also known as the place to go for a "how to" lesson in anything and everything.

Someone there will gladly teach you, or give you helpful advice, if you want to learn any kind of handwork or build a house, hang wallpaper, fix a leaking sink or some good ole' down to earth household keeping and cleaning hints, swap recipes or learn to cook, even how to take care of a fresh new hairdo by wrapping bathroom tissue around it or by sleeping in a pair of worn out underwear over your head (I've tried both and they work). Home remedies for the miseries or how to cure warts, change a tractor's tire, tune up a car or even fly an airplane.

All you have to do is just mention, "Does anyone here know how to ------," then sit back and take notes.

For the folks who are interested in becoming a member of the beauty shop's library and book club, the membership dues are one brown paper bag (grocery size) full of books donated.

And, there's always the homemade posters of coming events that cover the walls to read at a glance.

Then, for those people, like my son, who forgets their heads everywhere they go, for them I have the shop's lost and found department. While cleaning it out, I located my son, Marshall's head one day. Also my customers' forgotten belongings which include jewelry, handbags, a rubber ducky, eye glasses, wallets, a rotten jump rope, a plastic baby bottle and a chewed up pacifier, kids toys, sweaters, one corn cobb pipe, coats, umbrellas, keys, one tennis shoe and a blown out flip flop sandal, a man's toupee, a dirty shirt, an ugly rag doll, an assortment of hats, one hearing aide, and lots of different colored headscarves, plastic and cloth headbands, hair nets, ribbons, pins, bow, barrettes, a pair of work gloves with no fingers, a dog's flea collar, a few safety pins, buttons, needles, one false eyelash, a tube of lipstick, and somebody's pair of holey britches size unknown.

As I sat looking through all these forgotten things, I pondered about cleaning out this messy junk and having a giant garage sale. But then I remembered I still hadn't located the little old lady's missing set of false teeth in the lost and found department. I guess my garage sale will just have to wait until then.

In the meantime, if you pass by a beauty salon on a dairy farm with kids playing in the yard, honk your horn a hello. Or, if you have nothing better to do, stop in for a visit – unless, of course, the bull is running around loose that day. Then you had best keep right on truckin' by.

Chapter 16

THE COUNTRY CAMPAIGN HEADQUARTERS

There isn't a person alive that's more complimentary than a smiling, campaigning politician out to influence people and win votes before an election.

During a recent local election time, there were so many pieces of campaign literature piled all over the beauty salon for so many different candidates that I couldn't even find a comb and brush to use on my patrons.

One local candidate came in the shop to leave his bag full of paid political advertisements for me to hand out. This included 7 posters, 2 billboard signs, 83 small cards, 126 large pamphlets and 11 bumper stickers. I told him to put everything beside his opponent's stack of campaign material.

I made up my mind that very minute who I was voting for, as he was kissing my wet shampoo hands and telling me how beautiful I was, and how much he appreciated my support and, of course, the most important part, my vote! When he started to leave he said smiling, "Oh, by the way, your plants on the front porch need watering."

My favorite candidate gave me a tee shirt to wear while working in the salon. He figured I could do a little campaigning behind my styling chair. But, being the gentleman that he was, he didn't mention that my chest was hardly the billboard that could really show off that shirt, because he knew I would do my best.

The first time I washed my campaign tee shirt, it instantly disappeared, only to be discovered the next morning on my daughter Tina, being used as a nightie. I told her that my favorite candidate wouldn't appreciate her sleeping in my tee shirt. She asked me, "Why?" "Because there's no one in your bed that can vote for him."

With so much of an assortment of campaign material stacked all over the place and being a "waste not" person, I soon found many uses for the stockpile of papers.

The cards and pamphlets kept the customers busy while they were under the dryers.

The billboard signs out in the front yard, gave the birds a new target to practice on.

The posters inside the Beauty Salon covered the dirty walls and bullet holes in the front door, plus my customers got to look at the latest candidates instead of the latest hairstyles.

The campaign cards and pamphlets were great for writing down grocery lists, notes to myself, or excuse or tardy notes to school for my children.

The bumper stickers came in handy to keep my son's worn out clunker cars glued together. They also were taped over cracks in the beauty salon's walls and the windows to keep out the rain.

Each and every candidate told me, that if I should run out of their campaign material that all I would have to do is call and they would see that I was replenished immediately. They'd probably even supply me with enough for the next election.

My thoughts to their comments were to have a party and roast hot dogs over a huge paper bon-fire.

Chapter 17

OCCUPATIONAL HAZARDS OF A BEAUTICIAN AND A DAIRYMAN

We've come a long way, baby – in both the hairdressing and dairying professions.

Not so many years ago, (but in what now seems like a distant age), milk came delivered in glass bottles and only men patronized barber shops while only women went to beauty parlors. Now, there is the plastic milk carton and the unisex styling salon.

But, the one aspect that remains unchanged in both occupations is the milker in the milking parlor and the hairdresser in the beauty salon. Both stand on their feet for hours, sometimes with an aching back and wet hands, working to successfully accomplish their jobs.

One of several occupational hazards of being a dairy farmer is to be kicked or stomped by a loco milk cow.

I've found a few of the occupational hazards of being a hairdresser and salon owner (besides sore feet, back aches and brown stained fingernails) are a tired mind, employee vacations and sick leave time.

It is difficult to describe the loyalty shown to a hairdresser by their satisfied patrons. These faithful and loyal patrons will follow their chosen favorite hairdresser over hill and meadow to have them, above all others, style their hair.

Sometimes, the loyalty of these dedicated patrons is put to the test during their favorite hairdresser's vacation or illness, and they have to endure another hairdresser working on their hair.

However on the other end of the hair, the different hairdresser sometimes goes through another type of endurance test of their own in patience and perseverance.

Gloria's vacation time from the beauty shop was coming up soon and I had been begging her to please wait and take a vacation later. The day before her vacation was to start; I got down on my knees and begged her not to leave me alone with her customers again. "But I have already planned my two-week vacation and I can't change my mind now," said Gloria. She went on to tell me of her plans to go camping with her children.

I cautioned Gloria not to get lost in the woods, not to get too close to the water where she might drown, not to get snake bit, and not to get a terminal case of poison oak while trying to get away from her children. I told her in case she got tired of all the fun of roughing it in the woods she could always come back to work at the beauty salon to rest up. She said she would definitely keep my suggestions in mind.

The one thing I told Gloria to do was to be sure and tell all of her customers that she would be on vacation and for how long and that I would work on their hair while she was gone.

I said, "Promise me, Gloria, you will tell each of your customers this before you leave."

"I promise," as she crossed her heart to seal her promise.

Some of Gloria's customers don't like me (that's no secret) to even touch their hair. When I do, they get all bent out of shape.

As I remember, I found out how her customers felt about me the first time Gloria was sick and stayed home from work. I was working at Gloria's station that day as one by one her customers came in the beauty salon.

Mrs. Grass was the first to come in for her appointment. "Where's Gloria" she demanded.

"She's sick today so I'll set your hair," I said.

Mrs. Grass said stiffly, "Gloria can't get sick. She walks on shampoo."

Finally, Mrs. Grass, who had a dollar or two squirreled away, decided to let me touch her hair, since she was leaving on a ritzy 93-day around-the-world trip and didn't want to have her hair styled again until she returned home.

As I was busy shampooing Mrs. Grass' hair, I listened to her tell me that I didn't scrub her head as hard as Gloria did. She asked, "Now, what did you say your name was again?" (It's amazing how quickly they forget, because Mrs. Grass had been my customer for nine years before changing to Gloria.)

About that time another customer opened the door, took one look at me (she didn't' even finish coming in the shop, but stood in the doorway), and asked, "Where's Gloria?"

I told her, "She's sick today, so I'll style your hair."

She ignored the part about me styling her hair and asked, "When will Gloria be back to work?"

I replied that Gloria had called me early that morning and said she had the seven-week virus and if she felt better by then she would be back to work.

The woman in the doorway said she would just wait until Gloria came back to get her hair shampooed and set. With that statement, she slammed the door and the whole beauty shop shook.

While I was rolling Mrs. Grass' hair, I was saying, "Yes, I know I'm not rolling every hair like Gloria rolls it," when the phone rang. I thought a quick prayer, hoping it was Gloria calling to say that she had had a miracle recovery and would come back to work in five minutes. Instead of Gloria calling, it was another one of her customers to ask if the terrible rumors she had heard going all over town like wildfire were true.

"Yes," I told the woman, "Gloria is sick today and I am working her customers' hair." With that, the woman dropped the receiver without even saying goodbye.

While Mrs. Grass was under the dryer, Homer came for his appointment. He asked shocked, "Where's Gloria?"

I told him that Gloria was sick today, but I would gladly cut his hair.

As I cut Homer's hair, he kept saying, "That's not the way Gloria cuts my hair."

When I finished his haircut, well, I just hate to see a grown man cry. Finally, I told Homer that I thought his ears were cute and not to worry, his hair would grow back in a month or two. Besides, he could always wear his cowboy hat pulled down over his nose, until then, no one would know him.

My next haircut customer cried too, when I cut his hair. This one was a two-month old baby, who was the son of one of Gloria's standing customers. The mother told me the only reason she would let me trim the child's hair was because he was too young to know it wasn't Gloria on the other end of the scissors.

While I was finishing up with the baby's hair, he caught a glimpse of me and started crying and the mother said, "I was wrong; he does know you're not Gloria after all."

I signed, "Yes, Mrs. Grass, I know I don't comb your hair the way Gloria does." As I was teasing her hair with all my strength, she was gritting her teeth and tears rolled down her face. But I knew that I had to do a real job on her because she wanted her hair to last for the entire 93-day world trip she was taking.

I was putting the final touches on Mrs. Grass' hair style, when the phone rang again. I thought, maybe Gloria feels better and is calling to say her car won't start and she needs a ride to work.

The caller was my mother. She had called to visit with me over the phone while I worked.

I started to tell Mother about Gloria being sick, as I sprayed hair spray and Final Net on Mrs. Grass' hair for the 13th time to make sure that her hair wouldn't dare move out of place on her trip.

Continuing to talk to my mother on the phone, I decided to take her suggestion to hang a sign on the front door of the beauty shop the next time Gloria was not there. It would read, "Gloria's not here today." This would keep me from a lot of explanations in the future.

I said goodbye to my mother on the phone and thought I was finished with Mrs. Grass' hair – all the time telling her how beautiful she was – and, as she looked in the mirror, she said, "My hair doesn't look like it does when Gloria does it. She always puts a little curl on one side of my forehead and a half bang on the other side. Gloria knows exactly how I like my hair styled."

I said, "Mrs. Grass, I did the best I could with the three hairs you have on your head. Besides, I think your hair looks just like the picture you brought in to show me of the movie star's hair style that you wanted."

Mrs. Grass shook her head and said, as she paid me for her shampoo and set, "My hair just doesn't look the same as when Gloria styles it."

As she was leaving the shop, dear sweet Mrs. Grass announced loudly, "The next time I have an appointment with Gloria, tell her she can style my hair first, then go home and be sick on her time and not mine."

When Gloria came back to work after her illness, I told her how bad her customers had acted about me working on their hair. She said, "That's nothing. When you're sick and your customers drive in the driveway and see my car parked out front instead of yours, they just back out and leave without a word."

Late in the afternoon before Gloria's vacation started, she said to me as she was getting ready to leave, "I've told all of my customers, like I promised that I'm going away for two weeks and that you would be working on their hair while I was gone. A few said they would be nice, but I don't know how the rest of them will behave. They remembered the last time you 'touched' their hair when I was sick."

"Your customers will just have to put up with me or go dirty-headed for the next two weeks," I replied.

Now I know why Gloria always makes sure I keep my promise to tell my customers when I'm not going to be at the shop... although, I think the nice customers far outnumbered the mean ones.

After Gloria left on her vacation that day, I decided to be on the safe side so I hung the sign on the front door of the shop saying,

"Gloria's not here today." Standing back with a smug look on my face, I thought, "That should take care of the customers she forgot to tell."

Chapter 18

THE FORGETFUL BOOSTER CLUB PRESIDENT

One Wednesday morning I was giving my regular 10:00 a.m. customer, Gundella, a permanent wave. As I wrapped her hair in permanent wave rods, I told her how the pressures of being President of the school Booster Club were getting to me early in the term and affecting my tired, feeble mind.

As Gundella flipped the pages of a movie magazine and pigged-out on a box of animal crackers, she just half-listened as I told her my story.

"Yesterday, I went to the election poles to vote. I went inside the building, and announced my name, 'Frances, with an "E", seven times to the women who were sitting at the registration desk drinking coffee and talking. Finally, I got their attention and told them my name was not like the talking mule's, but the same as the November Hurricane.

The women and I were so amused over my clever little name dropping funny, that we all laughed. Then, one of the women gave me a slip of paper and told me which booth to vote in, and I handed my slip of paper to a fat man with a burr haircut sitting beside the booth.

Inside the voting booth, I stood there reading the ballot, and then tried several times to pull the lever to vote. Nothing happened. Then I used both hands to pull the darn lever down, thinking I might break the machine from pulling so hard. Still, nothing happened.

I was still pulling with all my strength when I noticed a woman's voice from the desk saying, 'Frances,' over and over again. I still didn't know she was talking to me, because after years of being called, 'Frances, the talking mule,' I now only answer to the name of Fran.

Finally she said loudly, 'Mrs. Powers, do you need assistance in closing the booth's curtain?' That got my attention.

After I closed the curtain, I pulled every lever that would then move. I felt like the number one country bumpkin of the day and ran straight toward the snickering woman at the desk."

Gundella laughed, "I bet that was funny."

"But that's not all," I said. "While Hughes and I were eating lunch, he asked me who I voted for. I told him I didn't remember. He said that was the stupidest thing he had ever heard. Then I told him about the bout with the booth's curtain and then he had a good laugh, too."

Gundella stuffed another animal cracker in her mouth and asked, "Who did you vote for, anyway?"

I told her the same thing as I had told my husband. To this day, I don't remember who I voted for, and if any of the candidates would ask me if I voted for them, I'd say, "Sure, I did."

My customer giggled and said, "Fran, you're crazy."

"Yes, I know. You don't have to keep reminding me. But just a minute. That's not all of my story about the pressures of being Booster Club President, and what they are doing to me."

I continued to tell my story to Gundella, as she dozed off and on.

"Yesterday was my day off from work, and I spent the usual day at home. The day went by so fast and before I realized, it was about time to go to the Booster Club Open House at school. Suddenly, I realized that I hadn't even written my welcoming speech.

I mentally started writing my speech while I cooked supper, more while we ate, and more when I was feeding the animals, and still more while I washed the dishes. The speech got a few more sentences as I was putting my clothes on. The most important part was added when I put my shoes and combed my hair."

"Gundella," I snapped, "Are you listening?"

"Yeah," she yawned.

"I left the house first, thinking Hughes would bring Tina to the meeting with him.

After I arrived at the school, I was busy visiting with all the people. Gundella, do you know what a madhouse a cafeteria full of football and volleyball players, along with two squads of cheerleaders, plus all of their parents is like?"

She nodded her head up and down.

"The parents were walking around visiting while the football and the volleyball teams continued their practice and while all of the coaches were yelling and blowing their whistles. This gave the cheerleading squads the spirit so they started practicing their cheers.

I was doing my best to count noses, so I would be sure there would be enough punch and cookies for everyone. I guess I counted wrong because after the football team finished serving themselves, there wasn't anything left but cookie crumbs and empty punch cups.

The principal called for quiet and then introduced me to everyone. And, would you believe what that man called me?"

Suddenly Gundella gasped and in a shocked voice said, "Oh no, not a dirty word in front of all those children."

"Worse than that. He referred to me as *your* president," I said.

My customer said, "Well, that's not so bad. After all, you are the Booster Club president, aren't you?"

Just then, I started to put the cold permanent waving lotion on Gundella's hair and told her to stop wiggling and squirming even though I knew the waving lotion felt like worms crawling over her head.

She remarked, "What price beauty," as she wiped off the excess waving lotion that had run down her face and into her ears.

I said smiling, "Remember, Gundella, the old saying, we'll go through anything to be beautiful."

With this thought in mind, I set the timer for the permanent wave to process and then asked my customer, "Don't you want to know why the principal called me '*your* president' instead of '*our* president'?"

She said, "Because there were no cookies or punch left for him?"

"You're probably right. That could have been part of the reason," I said. "But I think it was when I stood up in front of all those people that just sat there with their mouths' wide open and stared while I gave my ad-lib speech, because after I finished my welcoming speech was the time when the principal started with the '*your* president' bit to everyone.

After the many goodbyes and goodnights to the folks, the principal walked up to me and commented, 'What happened to your welcome speech?' I told him, I couldn't remember where I had put it or what I had said in the dang thing, so I had to ad-lib. He grunted and shook his head, then said, 'I know. We all noticed.'"

Finishing my customer's permanent, I was rolling her hair in curlers as we continued our conversation about the problems of being the forgetful Booster President due to the pressures of the office, when Gundella said, "Fran, remember last year you said, 'no more club work' of any kind? You said that you weren't doing one more thing. You swore an oath, and gave the cross-your-heart-and-hope-to-die-sign to prove it." (My customer had to be a smart aleck to bring up all those old oaths.)

I said with a shrug, "No, I don't remember saying that; was I well that day?

But let me tell you what really finished off the Booster Club day It was after the meeting and open house was over," I said.

"Hughes came up to me and asked, 'Where's Tina?' I told him that I didn't know, I hadn't seen her. Hughes started to run to look for her while I cleaned up the mess in the cafeteria.

He came back in a few minutes and asked me again, 'When was the last time you saw Tina?' I told him, 'I think I saw her after you got to the open house.' He said, 'I have looked everywhere and can't find her.'

Well, that did it – you know a mother hen I am over my children."

Gundella said dryly, "How could I forget, when that is all you ever talk about during my Wednesday appointment?"

I snapped, "Do you want to hear the rest of my story or not?"

Gundella grinned, "Might as well, since I can't leave yet."

"I told Hughes to search the parking lot and the football field, while I looked in the gym and the principal's office. He then started a search through the other school buildings. The parents that wanted to visit were told that I had to search for our lost daughter, and they all volunteered their help to find Tina.

The next place I headed for was the sidewalk in front of the cafeteria, and did what any mother of a lost kid would do, call the kid's name. "Tina, Tina, where are you?'

I looked in the gym, no Tina. Went through the boy's restroom looking for her. I found Hughes, but no Tina.

I was really upset this time, along with all the terrible thoughts that went through my mind. Hughes had looked every place, and still no Tina.

We had looked everywhere and I started to cry and said to Hughes, 'Where can she be?' He asked me, 'Did she ride with you tonight?' I said, 'No, I thought she rode with you.' 'No, she didn't' ride with me either.'"

Gundella was all ears at this point and she asked me to tell her where Tina was. "Well," I continued, "Poor little Tina was home all the time. We had both taken off, thinking she was with the other, and forgotten her at home."

"Sounds to me like the pressure of your office are getting to your family, too," stated my customer.

I had to agree with Gundella. But I didn't tell her I had forgotten to put the neutralizer on her permanent wave. But next week I'll correct it, I thought to myself, if I don't forget, because I forgot to finish my story about the part where one of the Booster Club members called on the phone in the middle of the night and asked me what the election returns were and if my candidates were winning.

At this point, I heard my customer's voice from under the dryer interrupting my thoughts. Gundella said, "Wouldn't I dry better if the dryer was turned on?"

As I turned the hair dryer on, my next customer, Lucia Sue, walked through the door. I looked surprised to see her and the thought hit me that I had done it again. I had forgotten to write her name in the appointment book.

I said, "Good morning," as I ran past her to the desk to write her name down in the appointment book. I looked at the book and discovered that I had not forgotten this time, but Lucia Sue had. Her appointment was for last week, not this week.

Just then the lights went off in the beauty shop which suddenly made me remember that wasn't the only thing I had forgotten about yesterday. I was so busy, I had forgot to go to the bank and deposit the dairy's milk check and then stop by to pay the electric bill for my beauty shop and the dairy farm!

Chapter 19
THE GODMOTHER

"A woman's place is in the home," mumbled my husband one morning as he stood looking at the crop of green fuzzy hardened leftovers inside the refrigerator.

'What's this?" he asked, taking a big bite out of a leafy object he picked off a shelf. Before I could stop him, my husband swallowed the object, then said, "Whatever it was, it sure lost its pizazz."

I said softly, "That was my last year's Mother's Day corsage."

My husband picked the dried flower petals out of his teeth, walked out of the kitchen in a huff, and said over his shoulder, "I'll bring my pitchfork home from the barn so you can use it to pitch out all that old stuff inside of the refrigerator."

I thought, "Why, on my day off from work, do I have to clean out that dirty foul-smelling creep?" This was a job that I could always put off just another day or week, but I decided today was the day to tackle the job I had been putting off since I attended Beauty School twenty years ago.

I had my head inside the refrigerator calling, "Come out, come out, wherever you are." I had a thought that the kids' friends were hiding in there waiting for me to run them home. My children always stand at the refrigerator with the door wide open, continually calling their friends' names. "There's nothing to eat." They are in the habit of doing this wherever they can find a refrigerator.

I was halfway into the fridge when the phone started ringing. After getting to my feet, knocking my head on a shelf, and gathering my thoughts together, I answered the phone and Gloria at the beauty salon said, "Fran, guess what?" (Well, twenty questions wasn't my idea of getting the gruesome task done that I had started.)

"What do you mean; I'm going to be a godmother again?" I shrieked. This news was the three-minute heart stopper. In fact, I suddenly forgot what I was looking for in the refrigerator.

When I composed myself enough to speak, I said, "I should have known better years ago, so this wouldn't have happened."

Gloria, in a very puzzled voice said, "What was it you should have known?"

I said, "To have hired a male hairdresser. I'm getting too old to be a godmother again."

"Gloria, are you sure?" I asked.

"Yes," she said. "I'm sure, and the baby is due in three weeks. Haven't you noticed my figure change AND my stomach resting on the shampoo bowl during working hours?

"No, I hadn't noticed. I just thought you had a case of indigestion from eating all of those pizzas covered with ice cream and pickles for lunch lately.

You said the baby is due in three weeks? That doesn't give me much time to work on your customers' hair again. Then it hit me – that means I'm really going to have to work on your customers' hair again!" This thought made me want to hide inside the refrigerator for the next twenty years.

"Gloria, I know your tips haven't been the greatest lately, but really, getting pregnant to increase your tips is ridiculous."

I said to her, "Promise me that you will have the baby between shampoo and sets or on Sunday so you won't miss work. Better yet, if you can arrange to have it between shampoos, I'll even deliver it in the storeroom, 'cause you know that I have a little experience with new births (that is, delivering baby calves). Being a dairy farmer's wife has widened my education on many things. I know that we could find the things we need right there in the shop."

Of course, Gloria didn't think this was the best of ideas. She said, "When the time comes, we will probably be out of hot water, or you won't be able to get your rubber gloves on, or the mouse in the back room will have eaten the last spool of thread. And, by the time you find your pair of scissors, the baby will already be born and old enough to start to school."

"That's true," I said, "So plan on having the baby on Sunday."

Gloria said excitedly, "Tomorrow, I'll have to make the announcement to the customers at the beauty salon so we can get some ideas for the "Name the Baby Contest" and then added before she hung up, "Have a nice day."

As I sat on the floor holding the phone receiver, I slowly went into shock over her news. Suddenly the thought sunk into my numbed brain. I said to myself, "Godmother again. Why me, Lord, when I have such a hard time remembering children's' birthdays? Now there are three God-children to mix me up more!"

The next day after Gloria had made her big announcement about her new noticeable condition to our customers, all the excitement began. I must admit, there's something about an expectant mother that brings out the maternal instincts in people. The ladies began knitting and all the other handwork that they could be doing while they were sitting under the dryer. Then, there were the untalented folks like me that went out shopping for the needed things for the new baby and mother.

Also, after Gloria's news, there was a massive amount of birth and rebirth stories as told by our customers; a complete description from first labor pain to the last after birth pain.

I noticed Gloria's tips did increase tremendously during her pregnancy. I know things like this happen, having been that way myself a few times after my dog ate my pills.

Everyone got into the "Name the Baby Contest." First prize was getting to feed the baby for one full week, including burping, and after each feeding, a new diaper change.

The tension was mounting in the beauty shop as a new entry would enter the contest. Time was growing short and names were getting to be many.

Debbie submitted her contest name entries of "Sir Michael," after her husband's name, and "Niki", after her dog's, of course.

Hughes' mother, better known as Mother Powers, who like myself mothers everything and everyone, has an interesting habit of announcing her arrival in the beauty salon with, "I'm the mother-in-law." One day she stated, matter-of-factly, the names of Bertha and Hubert for the baby.

One of Gloria's male patrons kept insisting his entry of "Lady Godiva" was a sure-fire winner.

Naturally, I was counting on my favorite to win – "Frivolous Dawn," or "Missy Clairol" if it was a girl, and "Willie Joe" or "Elmer Lee" if the baby was a boy.

The big day finally came, like all the better plans of dairy farmers of not mixing together dry cows with the milk cows. My plans of the baby arriving on a Sunday worked out the same way. Our baby picked a Saturday instead, and came in not with a name from the contest but with the name of "Baby." Gloria had decided this would keep all of our customers from being disappointed and would fit him fine for a while.

Most of our customers are experts on mothering, not only their own children, but Gloria's and my children, as well.

I proudly announced to everyone as they come into the beauty salon for months after, that "I am the baby's Godmother."

Chapter 20

WHAT'S HAPPENING IN THE "SOAPS" AND NOT IN THE SHAMPOOS

People often as me what folks talk about while under the hair dryer at the beauty salon. And I usually tell them that conversations in the shop cover everything from the cow that jumped over the moon to anything under the sun.

What's happening in the soap opera stories is one of the main topics of conversation among everyone at the beauty salon but me. From years of living and working in a live TV-soap opera atmosphere, I got to the point that I couldn't tell the difference between my own real life adventures and the ones in the stories I am watching.

I am now a charter member of the "Kick the soap opera viewing habit." There is only one TV show I refused to give up when I joined the group.

Every morning, I look forward to watching my all-time favorite with the star that is my heartthrob. I have had a thing for this star for years. I just couldn't start my day without watching "My Captain," and any man that wears "green jeans" is definitely my kind of man, also.

The Beauty Shop's TV Soap Show experts are Gloria and Debbie and my son, Chuck. Debbie and Gloria bring a portable TV to the shop so they won't miss what's happening on their favorite shows while they work on their patrons.

This usually delights the "addicted" patrons, except when they happen to want to watch a different soap on a different station.

During these times, I leave the refereeing to Gloria and Debbie to fight out who gets to watch which program. I really don't care what they watch as long as I don't have to listen to it over the arguing of the patrons. Besides, I don't want to miss hearing a single word from the customer I'm working on who is describing every detail of what's happening in their own real life story.

I've often pondered where I went wrong with my son, Chuck. He has become the worst TV soap "addict" of the group.

Chuck started his daily viewing habit when he went off to college. His explanation to me was that he started very casually while on the football team at college. The rest of the world did it, so he thought he may as well go along just for the fun.

From what Chuck tells me, it not only seems to give the team something to talk about besides football play and girls, but they all think it keeps their spirit up when they are all together in front of the boob tube.

There are times when Chuck will come into the beauty shop for one reason or another (usually to ask to borrow money or my car), and one of my customers will ask a question about the soaps. If Gloria and Debbie aren't there, I refer them to Chuck, and everyone seems happy as they go into detailed descriptions about this one or that.

I don't know a quicker way to make new friends and get a conversation going than to mention that you watch a certain serial on TV.

The other day while I was braiding Mrs. Fan's floor length hair into a Bo Derek look, Chuck and Mrs. Fan became hard fast friends. They were so deep in conversation about their soapy shows that they didn't even know that I existed. After I had finished with the braiding, it suddenly occurred to me and I asked Chuck, "You mean that I am paying for you to go to college to get a degree in "Soap Opera?"

I must have struck a nerve or rang a bell, because he didn't answer my question or even ask to borrow the car or money. He simply made a quick running exit out the shop's back door.

Not being a "Soaper" makes it difficult when a customer comes in and wants her hair done like this actress, "Greta's" or like "Monica's." And, when you can't relate to the customer, it makes for a frustrating day. I usually ask her what soap she watches and at what time of the day. Then, I try to find one of the groupies who watch that show and have them describe the hairstyle to me so my customers can be happy. At times, it cannot only become annoying, but also very costly.

Mrs. Fan came in for her regular appointment the next week. After I finished her shampoo, I combed through her wet long tangled hair. She remarked, "I'm tired of the Bo Derek look; I keep tripping over my braids all the time. I want a new hairstyle, something short and easy to take care of. You know my friend, Emma; she has one of those permapress, wash and wear hairdos. All she had to do is just wash and go.

"No," I mumbled, "I don't know your friend, Emma," as I got down on my knees combing her hair.

Mrs. Fan thought a minute, then said, "I know how I want my hair cut and styled; just like the hairstyle on the actress on my favorite TV soap opera show has."

She looked at me sitting on the floor covered with her wet hair and asked, "Do you know what the actress' hair style looks like on my soapy show?"

I thought, "Oh no, here we go again." Then I asked her what the name of it was and what time it came on and thought I could get an idea from one of my other operators.

This seemed to satisfy her until I asked Debbie and Gloria and neither one of them had ever watched Mrs. Fan's soap show.

Finally Mrs. Fan said, "I know who else watches my favorite TV soap show. Your son, Chuck, does."

"But Mrs. Fan," I said, "He's away at college now and that means I would have to call him long distance to ask him what the actress' hair style looks like. Besides," I continued, "it takes an act of Congress and a National State of Emergency to get him to the telephone at his college."

Mrs. Fan persisted, "Won't you at least try and get a hold of him? It shouldn't be that much trouble. I'm sure Chuck can describe the actress' hair style to you far better than I can."

As I dialed the long distance operator to place a person-to-person call to my son, suddenly lesson number eight from Beauty School popped into my mind. "It's a jungle out there. Be prepared to meet all kinds."

After I gave the operator the number she came back on the line and said there was no listing of a Chuck Powers at that college. I yelled, "Operator, what do you mean no person by that name? I'm his mother and I am sending the checks to that college for someone to attend there and it better by my son."

After that statement, the operator said before disconnecting, "Please call the college number direct."

I then dialed all 13 numbers plus the area code of the college and waited for the call to go through. Finally a voice came over the receiver and said, "The number you have dialed is no longer in service. Please try your call again. This is a recording."

Mrs. Fan sat in my styling chair wrapped in a blanket of long wet hair patiently waiting for me to get the call through to Chuck.

After I finished the third try and the recording said, "All circuits are busy. Please try again," I was starting to get a might upset, to say the least.

On the fourth try, "bingo," a woman's voice said, "Hello, may I help you?"

I asked quickly, "Is this the college? I want to speak to my son, what's his name. I mean, Chuck. Yes, that's his name."

The woman asked in a husky voice, "Is he a student here?"

I snapped, "Yes, lady. I have the cancelled checks to prove it."

"Who did you say was calling?" she asked.

"His mother," I answered dryly.

"Hold on one moment while I put your call through."

"That wasn't so bad, I thought. Only four tries and one hold later I'll get to talk to Chuck without getting an Act of Congress passed or proclaiming a National State of Emergency.

Twenty-two holds later, I had talked to five secretaries, three professors, four coaches, one cheerleader, seven basketball players, nine football players, the entire college marching band, plus the majorettes and the flag girls.

The next person I heard on the phone was a man with a very stern voice who asked, "May I help you, Madam?

I shouted into the receiver, "Don't madam me, whoever you are. If you don't find my son and tell him that his mother wants to talk to him right now, I'm going to call the President of the College and give him a piece of my mind."

The deep voice said, "Madam, I *am* the President of the College. Now, what seems to be your problem?"

After that earth shaking announcement, I humbly said, "Mr. College President, Sir, Your Highness, would you pretty please with sugar on it find my son Chuck and tell him that his mother needs to ask him a very important question. You will no doubt find him goofing off in the gym or in one of the girls' dormitories fooling around."

After the college president put me on hold again, I busily entertained myself by swatting flies in the beauty shop for the next 26 minutes.

"Hello," came my son's panting voice.

"Chuck, this is your mother."

"I know," he said breathless. "In fact, everyone on the campus knows. Every person I passed told me that my mother wants to talk to me."

"Well," I asked impatiently, "where were you?"

My son said, "I was in the girl's dormitory visiting and happened to be right in the middle of the most exciting part when I heard the College President yelling outside the building, "Chuck, your mother's on the phone and says it's an important National Emergency question she needs to ask you.

Mom, what's so important that you called me in the middle of the day about?"

I said, with a motherly tone, "First, young man, what are you doing that took so long while I waited for you to answer the telephone?" On second thought, I told my son to forget I ever asked that dumb question.

"Do you remember my customer with the floor length hair?" I asked.

"No, I don't know her," said my son.

"The customer that was in the beauty shop the day you came in to borrow my car and the two of you got involved in a conversation about your favorite TV soap opera and all of the characters," I reminded.

"Yeah," he said, "I remember now. What's the matter? Did she miss one of the programs and now wants me to bring her up to date on what's happening?"

"No," I said. "Mrs. Fan wants her hair styled like one of the actresses in that story and wanted me to call and ask you to describe it."

He asked, "Which actress is it?"

"Just a minute, I'll ask."

"Chuck, Mrs. Fan said the one with the red hair."

He gasped, "Ugh. I think she's gross ugly."

I said irritably, "Never mind how homely she is. Just tell me how her hair is styled. This phone call is costing me a large fortune."

Chuck thought a second, then said, "That actress has the same hair style that a girl in my English class has, or maybe it's like the boy who is in my P.E. class wears his hair now."

I snapped, "That helps a lot. I don't know what those people look like at your college. Can't you tell me someone I've seen before that has the same hairstyle that Mrs. Fan wants?"

I could hear the wheels turning on the other end of the phone but no words were coming out.

Finally, I hollered, "Chuck, for crying in a milk bucket, tell me the hair style I'm looking for before I have to pay the telephone company installment payments for the rest of my life for this call."

He answered softly, "I'll tell you, if you promise to send me money in the next mail out today."

I answered testily, "Consider your money mailed, and tell me."

"Ronald McDonald!" I repeated Chuck's words in shocked amazement.

"That's who I want my hair cut and styled like," mumbled Mrs. Fan, still hidden under her mop of wet hair. "The actress on my TV soap program and Ronald McDonald must be twins, because they look so much alike."

I hung up the phone and started to work on the new hairstyle that Mrs. Fan wanted.

Later, I had my own thoughts about having a "Big Mac" attack, but mine was not the kind to be eaten under the golden arches. Instead, it was the kind of "Big Mac" that might be driven right through the beauty salon where Mrs. Fan sat under the plastic hood of the dryer chair.

When I received the phone bill for the call to Chuck, I decided it would be cheaper to buy a TV and watch the soaps rather than go through another frustrating day like that one.

Better yet, I thought, the next time I'll charge the call to the dairy phone number, then tell my husband it was one of his heifers that had reached out and touched someone with her hoofs long distance.

Chapter 21

"DR. FRAN'S" HOLIDAY RUSH SEASON DIET

Diets are a popular subject in beauty salon conversation. Since I am starting the "going up the hill and over" age, (that's the age when the bag boys in the super market stopped flirting with me), I am interested in the latest diets, who's on one, who's planning to go on one, and who needs to go on one. There are as many new diets written as there are fleas on a dog after a long dry spell.

After years of having my own favorite, proven-to-work diet, I have not heard of one that works better. So, when my customers ask which diet I like best, I tell them that it is "Dr. Fran's Holiday Rush Season Diet." It works where other diets fail. I swear by it, and you don't have time to worry about your hunger pains and your will power. I promise you will lose weight if you follow it faithfully.

They ask me to write it down and give them a copy so they can try it.

DR. FRAN'S HOLIDAY AND RUSH SEASON DIET
- (1)　Start with one beauty salon
- (2)　Pour in 8 hours a day, 6 days a week
- (3)　Add 30 customers
- (4)　Stir in 25 customers that say, "After you finish my hair, you can eat your lunch"
- (5)　Mix in a holiday
- (6)　Whip in a rush season
- (7)　Let stand in place for 6 months
- (8)　For a snack, you can eat the following only one time a day:
- (9)　Two permanent wave and papers spread with styling gel
- (10)　One cup of Final Net

After staying on this diet one day at a time for six months, you will notice a difference in your body shape. Your backbone will be where your stomach started out.

Oh, I forget the most important ingredient – one Angel of Mercy.

Years ago, I would have starved to death standing behind my styling chair if it hadn't been for my Angel of Mercy customers.

These are the ones that feel sorry for their hairdressers' growling stomachs and say, "Eat your lunch first, then do my hair." Some of these Angels of Mercy even bring the ultimate blessing, FOOD.

After a while, our Angel of Mercy customers have their hairdressers well trained and spoiled. "Set up, Fran. Good girl. Now here's your cookie. Speak, if you want the cookie. Now, let's see if you can roll over and play dead."

Then, there are the customers that start to spoil me and all of a sudden, they are too busy to bake. That's when I munch on their hands and they soon get the message.

Not long ago, I suggested to Hughes – who plans to start his diet every Monday morning of each week—that he should try my diet plan. I explained it had worked miracles for the beauty shop customers that had used it.

My husband looked at me as if I had gone bananas, and then said, "I'd rather eat dry cow feed instead."

Chapter 22

WHAT'S A FEW MORE KIDS, ANYHOW?

There was an old hairdresser
who worked in a shop,
she had so many children,
who said, "there's nothing to do,"
that she finally went coo-coo.....

 What's a few more kids on the dairy farm or in the beauty salon? They're like barnyard cats. Having one more around wouldn't matter anyhow.
 My own kids hang out in the beauty shop and cruise around the parking lot in their beat up cars. It's a good thing we don't have an outhouse on the farm because my kids can't walk 50 feet. They would have to drive to get there.
 In a group of children, it's easy to pick mine out. They're the ones with the cowbells hanging around their necks.
 Time after time, I tell my kids to "close the beauty shop's front door," then ask, "Were you raised in a barn?" I don't exactly understand why my kids and their friends celebrate the 4th of July by exploding firecrackers in the yard on February the 9th while the shop is full of customers. They play cowboy and Indians using the beauty shop as the fort. Then they'll give an ear piercing "Tarzan of the Jungle" yell atop the trees in the yard. I holler out the window, "Get down before you bust your you know what."
 Each kid, in turn, will ask to borrow the use of my telephone, my bathroom, the curling iron, and hair blower. Then say, "By the way, Mrs. Powers, do you have anything to eat or drink in here?"
 Young folks will be young folks, I know, as I was one back in the good old days when dinosaurs roamed the pastures. But if I hear one more kid tell me a farmer joke, I'm going to commit Hari-Kari in the doghouse out back of the beauty shop.
 I get riled when the gang uses the dryer chairs for space rocket seats, and play elevator by pumping the hydraulic styling chairs up and down, especially when I'm working behind a patron that is sitting in it. That's the time when I fuss, or in their words, "get on their case".
 Keeping the shop equipment in place and in one piece is, to my

way of thinking, not making a mountain out of an anthill.

It's a shame that kids aren't born with good manners. Just think of all the trouble parents would be spared and the fun they would miss.

I have been known, at times, to get on my soapbox behind the styling chair and preach for hours on the subject of child raising. However, now I start my talks with the words, NEVER SAY NEVER. After I had to eat my own, never's for many a day.

With the beauty shop full of customers and young'uns, I never know what to expect.

"Boo, I got ya," a kid yelled from behind my back.

I jumped a foot, letting go of the shampoo sprayer hose. The kid looked shocked when the water hit him full force in the face. I smirked and thought, a drowned rat couldn't have looked better than him.

The phone rang. With a wet trembling hand, I answered it, wrote the woman's name down and left my signature on the appointment book with two shampoo bubbles and a watermark.

As I worked on a customer's hair, I listened to the crowd of kids in the next room having a bull session.

"What does a standing regular beauty salon customer mean?" one kid asked.

Some smart-mouthed kid answered, "Anyone knows that a Beauty Salon's patron is one that stands up while they have their hair done." Then kicking the bottom of the hair dryer chair with his shoe, he stopped a second and said, "I wonder how far a head cootie bug can jump?"

"I hope there's none in here," a girl said, scratching her head.

A little boy asked, while pointing to the spittoon in the corner of the room, "What's that used for?"

My son answered, "For mom's customers who enjoy a dip or a chew, while she works on their hair."

"For real?" gasped the little boy as he sat in the chair picking his nose.

A fat kid whispered to one of my kids, "Hey, I think your mother is getting mad. I hear her ticking. She must be a walking time bomb, and she's fixin' to blow."

"She just has a timer in her jeans pocket," said my son, flipping pages in a comic book.

One barefooted kid in cut-off jeans with his name written across the seat of them and no shirt on to show off the five hairs on his chest and who no doubt thought he was a macho man, laughed and said, "What does your dad use the corn he grows for – moonshine or gasohol?"

"Silage to feed our cows," answered my oldest son.

A boy asked my daughter, as he watched me working, "Does your mother always run around like a chicken with its head cut off?"

"Yep," she answered, between smacking her bubble gum.

"Is it true, that brown cows give chocolate milk?" asked a visiting city kid. Then with a shrug, he said, "Why's everybody laughing at me?"

I laughed so hard my ears hurt. Then I noticed my children and their friends giving each other quick, strange looks. With a devilish grin on his face, my third son said to the city kid, who was dressed in a white sports suit and wore shinning new white shoes, "Come on Jonathan, I wanta take you on a tour of our dairy farm and show you how the electric fence works, by touching it. I'll even give you a ride in the feed cart and take you for a walk through the cow lots. Then I'll show you how us farm boys really have fun with a little fresh mud.

"Can I ride on the tractor, pet the cows and climb in the hay loft in your barn?" asked the city kid, Jonathan, Jr.

Just then I interrupted their conversation by telling them to "move it," as I put a customer under the dryer.

I thought, "No wonder I have zits on my face, and at my age, of all things. It's gotta be caused from uptight nerves and not from eating chocolate Twinkies. I watched the gang of kids begin a tag football game in the dryer room, and then asked my customer to play center.

I told my kids to go visit their father at the barn and take their friends along, and to behave themselves, "and don't pull any tricks on that city kid."

Running out of the shop's back door, the fat boy shouted, "Last one in the pasture for a cow chip throwing contest is a rotten egg."

These are the times when I ask myself, "Why didn't I become a nun?"

After a day of working in the beauty shop curling my customer's hair amidst a nursery school of children who have run in and out of the door around and over my feet, my eyes bug out, my tongue hangs out, my ears constantly ring, and my head sprouts a crop of grey hair. Then my kids stare at me and say in unison: 'Momma, what big eyes you have."

I say, "The better to see my patrons' hair with, my dears."

"Momma, what a long tongue you have."

"The better to talk to my patrons' with my dears."

"Momma, what grey hair and wrinkles you have."

"My dears, if you know what's good for you, the better you didn't mention it. After all, you're the ones who put them there."

Sometimes, when they act so naughty, I would like to pinch their little heads off. That's when I snatch them up and go back of the wood shed for a heart to heart old-fashioned discussion. But, I quickly forgive and forget until the next time they drive me nutsy. Then they give me a hug and a kiss on the cheek and whisper in my ear, "I love you, Mother."

Of course, when I hear those magic words, my heart suddenly feels a warm glow, my eyes fill with tears as I softly answer, "Children, I love you, too."

Chapter 23

CONFESSIONS OF A WACKY HAIRDRESSER

After ten years of coming to the down-on-the-dairy-farm beauty salon, the customers slowly learned the deep, dark secret --- that my zany salon is different, and not the normal uptown beauty parlor.

I guess what let the cat out of the bag was the cow shocker hanging on a hook inside the supply room of the shop. And, the cattle crossing sign out front isn't the most typical for a beauty parlor parking lot.

But then, maybe the secret leaked out years ago when a big-mouth, gossiping busybody spread the rumor around town that the little smocks the patrons wore were really feed sacks.

Finally, I can't understand how that vicious rumor got started because I always cut the tags off and pull the strings out on each smock, then hide the evidence in the bottom of the trash can.

At times however, it does get boring to have to identify to the city slicker customers the various farm sounds and sights, as well as smells, in this "wildlife preserve."

Some days I feel like a tour guide working for a circus side show, with all of the questions of "What's that?" asked by the wide-eyed new folks that come into the beauty salon. What with the barn yard animals in the back yard, my next door neighbor's menagerie of pets (which includes a swinging bachelor rooster that only crows in the afternoon because he plays king of the hen house every night), my own litter's of different critters, plus my brood of four kids roaming in and out of the beauty shop, I'm kept busy answering questions and giving out detailed information about the feeding, care and breeding of each species.

When my four children are around the beauty shop, they like to get in their two cents worth of answering patron's questions. That's when my kids come out with their own mixed bag of kinky answers that sound like "close encounters with the fourth kind" which only adds to my premature senile condition.

The other day a real zinger came while I was cutting Ms. Brain's hair. (She was a new patron.) She was a know-it-all type and was on a bummer of an ego trip from the way she looked down at me over the top of her nose. As I cut section after section of her hair, I tried to impress Ms. Brain with my knowledge of hair, farming, and motherhood. All she said was, "Oh really," when suddenly my four siblings stampeded through the front door, covered from head to toe with mud, hay and manure (the remains of a recent cow paddy throwing match in the barn. The evidence was all over them.)

"Hi, Mom," said each kid as they marched single file by me to the bathroom, leaving a trail of stinky, yucky mess behind them.

Ms. Brain covered her nose with her hand against the aroma of my kids as they passed by her in the styling chair.

She asked me while making distorted faces, "Was that a chicken hawk that I saw perched on a limb in the oak tree out front of your beauty salon earlier?"

Before I could open my mouth, one of my children answered, "You saw a burkey in the tree, not a chicken hawk."

"A burkey?" asked Ms. Brain, with raised eyebrows and a hand over her nose. "What's that?"

I overheard one kid whisper to his brother, "Any bimbo knows what a burkey is."

"A burkey is a cross between a common breed of buzzard and a Thanksgiving turkey," said my child, the intellect, as he puddled the foul-smelling barnyard drippings on the floor.

After their display of smarts and my threats of tying them to the cow stanchions in the milking barn or washing their mouths out with shampoo, still hasn't discouraged the kids from visiting their Mama on the job.

My husband, Hughes, is not only the milkman, but the beauty shop and dairy farm's milkman, as well. It's his job to go to the post office, and then deliver the mail to its correct address. Sometimes, I think the pony express mailmen were faster. At least, they delivered the mail to the right address.

Hughes, being the modern day pony express mailman in his four-wheel drive pickup truck, frequently gets his dairy's mail mixed with my shop's mail. When this happens, my customers read the up-to-date dairy farming magazines and journals while they are under the hair dryers.

One lady told me, after she had finished reading an article in one of the dairy journals; "I guess it's the pull that counts in the dairy business."

While looking at the dairy magazines, some of the customers take special notice of the full page, color centerfold of the "heifer of the month." A few of the ladies will search out and hide the magazines with the "bulls for hire" pictures, then peek at them when they think no one is watching.

Meanwhile, my hairdresser magazines sometimes get delivered to the dairy barn and the dairy farm workers learn about the latest hairstyles and hair products, and look at the pictures of the hairstyle of the month.

At least one of the crew-members at the dairy farm enjoys reading my hairdresser magazines. Beth, the dairy's herdswoman, seems to know which trends are in even before I do.

You would think after receiving dozens of hairdresser magazines and journals, each one jam packed with articles and pictures of the latest beauty care products and hairstyles, that I would be satisfied. But no, not me. There's something about a magazine rack in a supermarket that I have a thing for. I just can't seem to control this uncontrollable thing I have.

First place I head for at the supermarket or drug store is the magazine rack. There I stand for hours flipping through the pages of the latest magazines or the newest books on beauty care and hairstyles. No matter how hard I try, my thing gets the best of me every time and I always end up buying one or two.

On these occasions, after I arrive home and come out of my trance, I ask myself, while looking at the books that I hold in my hands, "Where did these come from?" I don't remember buying them, then, "Oh, no," then I remember and whisper aloud, "My thing did it again!"

What to do with these books, races through my mind. Then, as always, I get the same brilliant idea. I sneak them in the back door of the beauty salon in the middle of the night and hide them on the tables beside the dryer chairs so no one will know about my "thing's" problem.

Not only do I have to cope with trying to keep hidden the problem of my "thing" but also keeping my imagination under wraps, for it seems like it's always running away with me. All it takes is a little something to set it off and running wild again.

I contribute the above mentioned personality disturbance to my twenty-odd years of sniffing hair sprays, listening to ringing telephones, tending livestock, inn keeping a boarding house, and driving a car pool to kids.

Watching the hair product ads on the TV seems to set my imagination off and running wild as a cattle stampede. Some of these TV ads are very entertaining. Every model shown has a full head of hair like a lion's mane. A young, pretty face to go with the hairstyle doesn't hurt either. And, you can be sure there is a paid professional hairstylist waiting in the wings, out of sight, to come and spray every hair on the model's head in place perfectly.

One morning while I was dressing to go to work, I watched an early morning TV show and one of the hair spray ads came on. During the 30 seconds that I watched the ad, suddenly, wham, ban, thank you ma'am, it turned my imagination on and running. I imagined how many products would be sold if the hair products were modeled by real people, like in the laundry soap ads, you know, the ones that wash their own hair. Or the type of woman that goes every place with her hair rolled in rollers and a scarf tied around her head.

Some of these roller head types of women are experts at rolling their hair. Their roller sets even look neater than mine. But when do they comb their hair out? Day in and day out they wear the same old rollers. Maybe they don't' have hair, but rollers, growing out of their heads instead.

At this point my imagination was running rampant as I could just visualize the TV ad using a roller head type for a model. With a can of hair spray in her hand and rollers in her hair, she says smiling, "Ladies, I just used Fluffy Brand Hair Spray on my rollers. It keeps my rollers in place after a busy day of chasing kids around, while working on my job at the car wash. Fluffy Brand Hair Spray keeps my rollers soft with the natural shining look. Just see how bouncy and manageable my rollers are! So ladies, if you want your rollers to look like mine, use Fluffy Brand Hair Spray today and have your husband tell you what beautiful rollers you have tonight."

Later that morning, with my imagination back to normal, I arrived to work in the beauty salon. It was also during a full moon cycle when everything acts crazy, myself included. I was busy working in the supply room of the beauty shop doing my mad scientist experiments. A new patron that had bleached and then used 47 different hair tints on her hair wanted a permanent wave. During the woman's precious appointment, I told her I would run a test on her hair first. So I cut a small piece off of her head to use. I told her that I would call her on the phone later about the test results on her hair.

I dropped a tiny piece of the hair in a cup of permanent wave solution. While I watched, I was fascinated by the different colors the hair was turning. While I held the cup up close to my face so I wouldn't miss seeing any change that was taking place, a woman with rollers in her hair came in the front door. Then I glanced at her, I knew instantly she was the roller head type from the telltale rust stains on her face, neck and ears. The woman, who looked as mean as a junk yard dog, asked me if I would comb out her hair, that she had a very important party to attend that afternoon. "It's a neighborhood window washing party," she excitedly exclaimed. I told her that when I was finished with my great experiment, I would comb out her hair.

After watching the piece of hair in the permanent waving solution take on a chewing gum consistency, I suddenly had an uncontrollable craving for a piece of chewing guy. Finishing my mad scientist test, I wrote down the results, and then called the customer, Mrs. Precious, to report her test results. "I will give you a permanent wave if you want to chew your hair instead of wearing it." With this done, I popped the piece of the newest flavor chewing gum into my mouth.

Then I told the woman with the rollers in her hair that I would comb out her hair now. She had the extra-large trash can size rollers in her hair, so I had to stand on a stool with a crow bar in my hand to start to take her rollers out.

I finally finished the job of removing the rollers with a chain saw. When I finished combing her hair with a yard rake, the woman couldn't believe that she was the same person that had come into the shop. She looked at herself in the mirror and exclaimed, "That's incredible."

I kept telling her over and over how beautiful she looked. She paid me for the comb out and said she was so pleased with her hairstyle that she wanted to give me a little something extra for doing such a fantastic job. This meant, to me, a nice fat tip. Instead, the woman handed me her bagful of dirty, rusty broken rollers and said, "Dearie, this is for you."

After she left the beauty shop, I thought, "Surely this isn't what old Mrs. Watson, my beauty school instructor, meant in lesson number three, entitled, "How to Become Rich and Famous" as I walked directly to the trash can in the supply room and deposited the rollers.

Later that afternoon I was working on my customer, Molly Parton, who was a dead ringer for the winner in the Dolly Parton look-a-alike contest – when a knock came on the beauty shop door.

Thinking this was a little strange, since there was a sign on the door saying, "Open, come in," Molly said sweetly, "Maybe it's the Avon lady." I said (to her), "My Avon lady never knocks. She just walks right in."

This ticked me off to have some ding-a-ling banging on the door while I was working on a patron's hair. The knocking continued to get louder and louder and gave me a case of heebie jeebies. I walked to the door to find out who the jerk was that couldn't read.

I opened the door and there stood a funny looking, knee-high sized kid dressed in a white rabbit costume. The kid wiggled his ears, and then said, "Trick or treat." I told the rabbit looking kid, "Just a minute. I'll get you a treat."

I walked to the backroom to look for something to give the kid. After a minute's thought, out I came carrying the only thing that I could find to treat with in the middle of the month of May. I handed the bag full of dirty, rusty, broken rollers to the rabbit looking kid and said, "Dearie, this is for you." The kid in the white rabbit suit, bag in hand, hopped off to the dairy's barn to play "Trick or Treat."

I slammed the door and said to myself aloud, "Really, with all of these crackpots and weirdo's running around, I'm going to tell my dinky boss to take this job and shove it."

That comment from myself, immediately got my full attention. I said to myself, aloud, "Hey, you are the boss." I answered myself sternly. "Yes, that's right, so don't call me a dinky."

"Dang it," I said to myself, "I'm doing it again, talking to myself all the time and now I'm answering myself, aloud too." Then I asked myself in a soft voice, "Do you think it could be caused from smelling permanent wave solution for all of these years, and now it's curling my brain?"

My whispered answer was, "Yep, I bet that's the cause or maybe it's from working in this beauty salon."

At that moment a case of cabin fever hit me and the urge to scream suddenly came over me. I ran out of the front door of the shop and let out a blood-curdling scream. Standing in the open doorway, continuing screaming, "Help, Help, I'm being held prisoner in here. Help me somebody help..."

The phone rang right in the middle of my healthiest "Help" scream. I decided the caller might be a customer wanting to make an appointment, so I calmly walked to the desk to answer the ringing phone.

As I picked up the receiver, I heard my husband's angry voice asking, "Fran, was that your customer I heard screaming a few minutes ago saying she was a prisoner and to help her?"

I said, "No, Hughes that was me."

"How many times do I have to tell you not to scream like that again," said Hughes. "It disturbs the cows."

I came back with a very sharp reply, "What do you know, the females that you work with all day don't talk, they just moo, and working in this beauty salon on a hectic day is like being in a nest of women having a non-stop hen party."

Hughes said, "But Fran, you should know that when the cows come out of the stanchions they jump into the feeding troughs." He added, "Even the milkers nerves are shot from listening to your screaming, while they have to dodge being kicked by the cows."

The farmer in me had to agree with my husband after all. I had forgotten that my screaming throws the cows' milk production off for weeks. And, it bothers the men milking in the milking parlor.

"I'll try to remember not to scream at work again, but will wait until I get home and use the back pasture to let loose in."

I hung up the phone, thus ending our husband and wife on the job conversation.

Then looking at my customer, Molly Parton, who wore a smock with tags and string on it, and had been sitting through the previous course of events without a word to say, "Now where were we before we were so rudely interrupted?" I asked her.

Expecting her to say, "Take me to your leader," she came back with an answer any spaced-out looking woman would use, with pieces of hair wrapped in foil sticking out all over her head like antennas on a newly arrived Martian.

I pulled the foil off of a piece of hair to check the bleach and see what color her hair was at that stage of processing. I decided, when in doubt, "punt" after seeing the color tone her hair had gotten at that stage.

"Was I icing or frosting your hair before we were interrupted?"

She quickly reminded me what I was doing to her hair, as I pulled each piece of foil off her hair.

Suddenly my customer, Molly Parton, giggles as she yanked the strings and tags from the brown smock she wore and said, "Hot damn! I can't wait to tell the girls in my bridge club about this beauty salon."

'T'IS THE SEASON OF INFLATION IN THE BEAUTY SHOP"

> T'was the day before Christmas and all through the shop,
> Not a creature was stirring, not even the lousy mouse,
> The stockings were hung on the mirrors with care,
> In hopes that our patron's tips would soon re-appear....

Chapter 24

"PATRON FOR A DAY"

Once a year, I go to a Beauty Salon as a customer, whether I need it or not. I enjoy sitting in the styling chair, instead of always behind one, having someone else doing my hair for a change. (I have heard waitresses say this about going out and not waiting on themselves. We're a breed of our own, aren't we?) A day at the other area beauty shops helps me remember how the other half lives.

Each year I pick a different salon to be a "patron for a day." This year's "lucky winner" was Mr. Tim's Uptown Styling Salon, the ultimate in the downtown, or uptown area. Making an appointment seemed to be a waste of time on the only day I could be on time myself, plus, I had to entertain myself watching the other hairdressers do the unpardonable sin of putting hairpins in their mouths (one of the "No No's" in Beauty School.)

After watching the goings on in this salon for what seemed to be an eternity (actually about 6 minutes), my name was called and I was led to the styling chair by a girl who said, "I'm ready for you."

Now this can have a dual meaning, and of course that's the way I took it.

I told her that I wanted Mr. Tim to do my hair. The girl laughed hysterically, and asked me who I thought I was? She said that Mr. Tim was booked solid for the next 3 years.

Well, why should I fuss? Zenda couldn't be that bad, even though she had been one of my former classmates at Doodly's in the good old days. In fact, we were the ones that took a recess when the "How to rinse hair, without drowning your patrons" lesson was given to the class.

Now, Mr. Tim's Salon was, once in a while, plagued with a low volume of water. This thought flashed into my mind when Zenda put my head into the shampoo bowl, so I yelled at Mr. Tim across the room and said, "Mr. Tim, if your water goes off again, I know a good Beauty Salon up the road that I would highly recommend."

With that statement out of my mouth, Zenda did the one thing that can jar you back into reality; she soaked me from head to foot with the shampoo sprayer. Poor Zenda, now I knew why she was given the award for, "The Slowest Learner in the History of the Beauty School."

After the shampoo and the "bath" were over, she graciously dried my clothes with a blow dryer, sat me up in the chair and said, "What look do you want?" I told her I didn't know what "look" I wanted.

Zenda, who had just squeezed me in and was 3 hours behind in her booking schedule, kept prodding me to "make up my mind." She finally said, "Well, do you want a classic, sophisticated, fun, chic, elegant, romantic, daring, exotic, sensuous, tailored, and sexy or something different like the "Total Baldness" look?"

I told her to give me the "combination".

After the rolling and drying time were completed, I excitedly sat in Zenda's styling chair to see the new me emerge from my "big day" at the beauty salon, other than my own. Five hours and 43 minutes later, she turned me around in her chair so I could see the "new me" look in the mirror.

I was shocked, dumbfounded and couldn't believe my eyes, that this was what I had sat for so long, seeing my hair was only an inch long to start with, all the time while Zenda was saying, "You look just beautiful, and the new look is really you." She went on to tell me she loved it.

My only comment concerning my "new look" after all of Zenda's hard work was, "Well, at least it's clean."

With that once a year visit to Zenda's at Mr. Tim's uptown styling salon, I discovered I really enjoyed having clean hair and the compliments that went with it. So, right then, I decided being a customer more often than working on one was definitely it for me.

The next time, the lucky winner I chose to be a patron was my own beauty salon, and with Gloria as my hairdresser.

I didn't call Gloria for an appointment. I just wrote my name in her column of the appointment book for Monday at 1:30 p.m. for a shampoo and set.

Monday came and I told my husband over lunch in a restaurant (this being both our days off we treated ourselves to a meal away from home), "Hughes, we'll have to hurry and eat. I have a hair appointment at 1:30 at my beauty salon."

He glanced at his wristwatch, slowly chewed his food and said, "Hum, it's 1:29 now."

Naturally this meal took longer than I had planned. When we arrived home, I rushed to the phone to call Gloria at the shop. She answered, "Fran's Beauty Salon."

Breathless I said, "Gloria, I'm sorry, I'm 35 minutes late for my appointment. Can you still take me? My hair is a mess and needs help."

She said testily, "You are late already and I'm busy right now."

I scratched my head and whined, "I'm sorry about being late, but I can come in a little later if that will help you out."

Gloria replied, "I have already made plans for later today. I have to pick up my kids from school, then go shopping and go over to my mother's house for her birthday party. I'm sorry I can't do your hair today. Why don't you call me tomorrow and make another appointment?"

After hearing the last statement, this disappointed dirty headed beauty salon owner told her hairdresser employee, "Gloria, tell your mother Happy Birthday for me, too." I hung up the phone and sighed, "Oh well, better luck next year," and scratched my head again.

I knew it was a waste of time to search through the house for a bottle of shampoo with a few drops left in it after my kids had shampooed their hair five times that morning. "Use this," Hughes said loudly, as he handed me a glass bottle that had a pretty label on it.

I thought to myself, "No doubt, I have married the most wonderful and thoughtful man in the whole wide world." But I reckon my opinion suddenly changed when I read the label on the bottle and came to the part that said COWDIP.

Chapter 25

BEAUTY SHOW OR COW AUCTION:
TO GO OR NOT TO GO, THAT IS THE QUESTION

When hairdressers or farmers get together in a group, first thing off, they both start to talk shop. I have attended both beauty shows and cow auctions. While there, I discovered that a Beauty Show is where the hairdressers go to let their hair down, and a cow auction is where farmers and ranchers go to tell yarns, swap lies and buy each other's culled cows.

I learned the hard way, long ago, what being married to a dairy farmer means when he says, "You wanta go?" That's when I have two choices. The first one is to go to the cow auction with my husband where all the action is; the second choice is to stay home on the dairy farm with his unexpected problems to bug me.

For instance, like the time the vacuum pump motor that runs the milking machines burned out...the automatic pellet feeder in the milking parlor broke down with the herd of hungry milk cows waiting to be fed... the milking crew didn't show up for work... the cows went through the fence during a lightning storm and got in the corn field... the milk tank compressor motor burned out during a heat wave... a first-calf heifer had trouble freshening... the electric fuses in the barn blew and, I guess, maybe I did too, after I went "bonkers" a few times and pulled my hair out from trying to manage the dairy farm.

Now, when I hear my spouse say "go", "A cow auction sounds good to me," is my reply. Then I run as fast as I can to his pickup truck climb in and lock the doors so I won't be left behind on the farm with the excitement that usually follows when my husband departs the old homestead. However, I also learned when I was just a blushing bride and still very wet behind the ears, there are certain motions a body just doesn't use while at an auction, or they end up buying the animal and taking it home.

"What in the sam-hill are you doing?" asked my husband irritably, while the auctioneer's voice blared over the loud speakers in the auction barn. Can't you see, I'm combing my hair," I yelled to him as I waved to my friend, Bobbie Jo.

"Sit still or you'll bid on that old dried up cow out there in the ring."

The auctioneer's voice roared, "Come on ladies and gents, what will you give me for this nice fat milking cow, what do I hear for her now? Who wants to open the bids?"

My husband remarked, "I bet that old heifer gives about a pound of milk a week."

I glanced at him and thought he looked kind of funny sitting on his hands and making weird faces.

"What's the matter with you?" I laughed.

"My nose itches," he said. "It's driving me up a tree."

I leaned over and scratched his nose and asked, "Is that better?" At that moment, the auctioneer nodded in my husband's direction and said, "Thank you sir for your bid."

"No, my nose still itches," mumbled my husband, as he watched me pull up and down on my earrings.

"Thank you, ma'am, for your bid," said the auctioneer, while pointing at me in the crowd.

"I can't understand a word that auctioneer is saying," I said to my husband as I patted him on the arm.

He shouted, "Fran, for goodness sake, be still or we'll end up buying that bag of bones and I'll be the laughing stock of the dairy farm."

Just then, I was tired and a little bored. So, I stretched one arm in the air and then the other one, folded my hands in my lap, after rubbing my chin a couple of times, and finally let out with a big yawn.

Suddenly I heard the auctioneer's voice ring out over the loud speaker, "Sold to the highest bidder."

Everyone clapped loudly as they looked my way.

The auctioneer pointed at me and said, "That little lady sitting over there wearing the tee shirt that says, "Get High on Milk; Our Cows are on Grass" is the proud new owner of this fine registered heifer."

My husband paled. I turned to him and asked numbly, "Does this mean what I think it does? That I have to pay for that poor skinny black and white polka dotted milk cow?" He nodded his head. "Happy Birthday, honey," I grinned.

Then my husband poked the old weather beaten farmer who was seated next to him, leaned over and whispered, "Ruford, I've never seen this ding-bat woman before in my life."

"Sonny," Ruford said, between chews and spits on a tobacco wad, "I know just how you feel. My misses bought a bull here once, and my only milk cow died the week before the auction and I sure as shoot'en didn't need no bull. From that day on, I leave my wife at the house. Might be a good idea if you did the same, young fella."

Needless to say, I'm glad my dairy farmer didn't take his advice.

Then again on the other side of the cow, I would like to remark here and now that Hughes has flatly refused in pig-simple language my invitations offered to him to darken the door to any of my hairdressers beauty shows.

My farmer husband tells me, "Going to a beauty show with you would be as useless as teats on a boar hog, or a bull in the milking parlor in my line of work."

"Just remember, dear," I tell him, "Dairymen and hairdressers both have great hands."

The tough part was to wear my husband's resistance down.

I tried pleading with him to change his mule headed mind. He only called me an old nag.

I even threaten to run over the television set with the tractor, before the Super Bowl football game, not to attend his family's yearly "gathering of the clan" reunion, to pack my bags and leave on a jet plane for a month's vacation and let him worry about cooking for the kids, cleaning the boarding house and feeding the critters. Still, he would exclaim, "A team of wild horses couldn't drag me to a beauty show."

Then I get down to the real nitty gritty plan.

As I recall, what finally changed my husband's mind one morning was when I bribed him with an exciting wifely surprise for later that night. Thank goodness, it works every time.

Silly me, if only I had thought about using that little trick sooner, he probably would have already gone with me to a beauty show. It seems my spouse just cannot resist his weakness for one of my delicious homemade apple pies for supper.

I said to him, "Before you change your mind, rush to the barn and check to see if everything is in tip-top running order. Don't forget to kiss your cows goodbye. You know how they pout when you forget."

"Yeah," he moaned, "They just get out of the fence and come looking for me."

Golly, to think my husband would attend a beauty show with me at last! I got goose pimples and broke out in a cold sweat from the excitement, and thought, "Just wait till my hairdresser friends meet him."

Houseflies on a piece of brand spank'n new flypaper couldn't have stuck any better than my beauty school instructor Mrs. Watson's words of advice have stuck firmly in my mind since graduation. With comb in hand pointing it at the class she would say, "Students, to keep up in the ever changing hairdressing profession, always attend beauty shows. If you don't, you'll get left under the styling chair instead of standing behind it."

As I was getting ready to go to the beauty show I thought, why is it every time I get gussied up in my high heeled shoes, dressed in my best Sunday go to meetin' clothes and sport'in a fancy hairdo (in fashion circles it's called the total look), that's when my kids take this as a clue that something's up and ask, "Where are you going?" Then they whine, "Can we go too?"

Once I'm out of my work clothes of jeans, tee shirts and nurse's shoes, is when the kids stare at me in shock, their own mother, as if I'm a complete stranger with a dress on.

"Gosh, Mother, you look neat," commented my daughter with surprise.

"Hey, Mom, I didn't know you had legs," remarked my son as he watched me practice walking across the room in a pair of high heeled shoes.

Just then, bumping into the wall, I asked him, "What did you think I used to stand on to work in the beauty shop - my hands? I'll have you understand these legs help keep you in peanut butter and tennis shoes."

At that moment the real kicker came when my middle child, the one with the five cow licks in his hair, walked into the room, stared at me in shock, then gasped, "French Toast, you really are a girl after all!"

How these kids think remains a mystery to me.

Later among the glitter and glamour of the beauty show, Hughes and I were seated on metal folding chairs. "This would make a real fine barn for the cows," my husband remarked, as he looked around the plush pink and blue ballroom with sparkling chandeliers hanging from the ceiling.

He mumbled, "Folks in here are packed tighter than sardines in a can."

"How do ma'am," he said to a woman, touching the front of his work cap with one hand and nodding his head.

Fluttering her false eyelashes, the woman asked him, "How are you handsome? What beauty parlor do you work in?"

He replied with a grin, "Fair to middling, thank you ma'am. I work in a milking parlor."

Just then I nudged him and said, "For God's sake, Hughes, did you have to wear your rubber boots?"

"Yes, unless you wanted me to walk into this place barefooted as a yard dog. My good shoes are being repaired."

Everyone but my husband waited patiently for Mr. Jud, the renowned world famous guest artist to get his act together and go to work on the platform in front of us.

I glanced at my husband who acted sorta antsy as he kept shifting his position around in the chair.

"Time flies when you're having fun," I said, as I scratched my head, folded the pleats in my wrinkled dress and looked across the crowded room for any familiar faces. There in that room it was quite apparent that hairdressers come in an assortment of shapes, sizes, and ages.

Finally, I spotted Mr. Tim and Zenda sitting in the far corner of the room and waved hello to them. I thought they looked tacky in their matching rhinestone urban cowboy outfits.

"He's cute," I remarked as we looked at Mr. Jud who was darting back and forth across the platform.

"He looks like a barnyard chicken chasing after a bug," commented my husband irritably. "When is that fella gonna get this show on the road? It'll be milking time before long and my cows can't wait on him forever."

Every pair of eyes in the room stared at my husband in disbelief. I thought maybe if I just ignore him, people will think I'm not with him.

I squirmed around in the hard as a rock metal chair in search of a more comfortable position for my then sore tush. While I twiddled my thumbs and thought there is a lot of truth to the old saying, "You can take the girl out of the country, but you can't take the country out of the girl."

Just then I decided what the heck, you only go through life once. Why not do it with gusto? I kicked off the tight fitting shoes that were killing my feet and slowly wiggled each numb toe. Then quickly decided I had better put the mean suckers back on after the woman who was sitting in front of me announced in a booming voice, "Phewee." That woke my husband up from his nap with a jolt.

At last the guest artist, Mr. Jud, bounced onto the platform in front of the waiting crowd. He wore a punk hairstyle and was dressed in a stunning skin-tight black outfit. I couldn't get over how many gold chains and diamond rings the man wore.

Suddenly, Mr. Jud ran his magic styling fingers through the model's hair with flair and started to dazzle us as we watched him work.

A hush fell over the crowd. One lady in the back of the room said excitedly, "Isn't he just fantastic."

My husband continued to snore more loudly while I sat with my back to him watching Mr. Jud's demonstration.

Mr. Jud combed the blonde model's sickly hair, winked at her and asked, "Hey, good looking, how about having a drink with me after the show?"

The model twisted in the chair and hid her red face behind her hands to giggle.

Mr. Jud continued to comb her hair between dropping his comb on the floor. He talked non-stop about hairstyles and fashion trends in foreign countries. He went on to tell a few corny jokes, then briefly informed us in a clever way that he thought there was a special place in heaven for hairdressers.

"AMEN," shouted the old timers as they agreed with him.

"Is it time to milk the cows yet?" asked my hubby as he opened one eye.

As I watched Mr. Jud madly pumping the hydraulic styling chair up and down, I suddenly began to feel sea sick green.

At that moment Hughes tapped me on the shoulder and asked, "Are you ready to go? This chair is harder than a tractor seat after a day of plowing the south forty."I snapped, "Not yet, Mister." "All right then, I'll read," he sighed as he sat fidgeting and pulled a newspaper from out of his overall's back pocket.

"Fellow hairdressers," yelled Mr. Jud, getting everyone's full attention. "I will now demonstrate for you the ultimate haircut." Everyone in the crowd strained their necks to get a better view of Mr. Jud's magic styling fingers at work. Everyone, that is, except my spouse who was reading the newspaper. With lightning speed, the world famous Mr. Jud used a tiny pair of scissors to cut a big hunk of the model's hair off. He held it up in his hand, then looked at the bald spot left on the model's head. "Uh-Oh," he gasped. That freaked the audience out as everyone roared with laughter and loudly applauded for more.

Just then Hughes leaned over and whispered in my ear, "Wow, that really is an ultimate haircut that fella did. Maybe I could get him to cut the cow's horns off for me." "Shhh, I might miss learning something from Mr. Jud."

My husband said dryly, "I've learned one thing at this beauty show from watchin' all these hair fixin' folks." "What's that?" I asked nervously. He said yawning, "Where the bar and restrooms are located."

"Gee, that's nice," I said with a shrug. "Listen to this," he said. I interrupted, "Before you start reading me the entire newspaper, I've already read it." My husband remarked, "You say that every morning when I'm reading the newspaper to you." He looked up. "Did you know there's a cow auction over in the next county tonight?" Then, with a crooked smile and a mischievous twinkle in his eyes, my husband asked, "You wanta go?"

It will be a cold day in August when cows fly before I invite that man to go to a beauty show with me again!

Chapter 26

WHICH JUST GOES TO PROVE

It was late on one of those days when nothing goes right and I wasn't quite sure why I even bothered to get out of bed.

The phone rang constantly, making it a real drag of a day. And, I was in the down in the pits mood when I felt unappreciated, overworked, underpaid, and still had more dirty heads and farm chores waiting for me.

Just then I could hear the discontented mooing of the cows at the dairy barn out back of the beauty shop. This meant the hungry cows would be served their well-balanced supper in the parlor and then milked. The impatient cows knew that bright and early the next morning came more of the same excellent service in the routine leisure life of a milk cow.

Which just goes to show that dairy cows aren't stupid. They know when they have it made. The more milk they give, the better the dairy farmer will pamper, spoil and wait on their every whim.

I just couldn't win. My standing customer, Mrs. O'Malley's hair wouldn't curl. It seemed she wanted a strange funky hairdo right out of a science fiction movie to wear to a masquerade party that night. Then, my kids called to ask, "When are you coming home to cook supper? We're starving, Mom!"

One by one, my four children had phoned me at work that day to tell me what disaster was happening at home – someone put the cat in the dryer, the dog left a big surprise for me on the carpet, there was no Band-Aids to stop bleeding with, or peanut butter, milk, or shampoo in the house, the washing machine was sick, it upchucked soap suds and water on the floor. And, of course, the tattle-tale reports of who punched hit and slapped who, so and so gave them a funny eye look, tell what's his name to stop calling them raunchy names. Finally, there was the "don't' tell I told you" report that half of the kids from school were having a party in our house. They were playing spin the milk bottle and having a food throwing fight and they planned to bring a cow inside the house to use for a mechanical bull ride.

As I hung up the phone after the last conversation with my kids, it suddenly dawned on me that my mother, with her infinite wisdom was right in what she told my three sisters and I after we had called her at work a few zillion times when we were aggravating kids. She always said, "Just wait till you have children of your own." Which just goes to say my mother really knew what she was talking about after all.

For the better part of an hour, I shampooed, conditioned, combed, teased, rolled, brushed, and sprayed Mrs. O'Malley's hair. Several times I closed my eyes and asked for divine guidance and lots of patience. Mrs. O'Malley didn't say anything, she only watched me flip through her hair and do my creative thing.

This inner voice was telling me what Mrs. Watson, my beauty school instructor, really meant in lesson number nine about hairdressing. It is not just a job, it's an emotion.

Finally, it was with a great sense of accomplishment that I viewed Mrs. O'Malley's hairdo and thought, not bad for an hour's work.

I must admit, although I may not be rich and famous, my greatest reward came when Mrs. O'Malley turned in her styling chair, looked into the mirror, tenderly caressed her new hair style and said – "I love it."

Before I could utter a heart-felt thank you to her, my husband rushed in the beauty shop's door breathlessly announcing, "Our cows are standing in the middle of the highway."

Which just goes to prove when you own a beauty salon on a dairy farm, you aren't your own boss at all. The *cow* is the boss.

The End